CW00473347

THE RAF'S FIRST JET SQUADRON

SQUADRON

616 (SOUTH YORKSHIRE)

THE RAF'S FIRST JET SQUADRON

616 (SOUTH YORKSHIRE)

AIR COMMODORE
GRAHAM PITCHFORK MBE, BA, FRAeS

Foreword by
DAVID MOODY ESQUIRE
The Lord Lieutenant of South Yorkshire

First published 2009

The History Press
The Mill, Brimscombe Port
Stroud, Gloucestershire, GL5 2QG
www.thehistorypress.co.uk

© Graham Pitchfork, 2009

The right of Graham Pitchfork to be identified as the Author
of this work has been asserted in accordance with the
Copyrights, Designs and Patents Act 1988.

All rights reserved. No part of this book may be reprinted
or reproduced or utilised in any form or by any electronic,
mechanical or other means, now known or hereafter invented,
including photocopying and recording, or in any information
storage or retrieval system, without the permission in writing
from the Publishers.

British Library Cataloguing in Publication Data.
A catalogue record for this book is available from the British Library.

ISBN 978 0 7524 4914 2

Typesetting and origination by The History Press
Printed in the United Kingdom by Henry Ling Limited,
at the Dorset Press, Dorchester, DT1 1HD

CONTENTS

FOREWORD

DAVID MOODY Esq
Lord Lieutenant of the County of South Yorkshire

The young men of South Yorkshire have never been slow to answer the call to arms when the need has arisen. The gallant deeds of the soldiers who fought in our local regiments and those who sailed in HMS *Sheffield* have been recorded over the years in several books, but the exploits of our airmen, those who served in South Yorkshire's own Royal Air Force squadron, have never been related in detail.

Now, a native of the county, Air Commodore Graham Pitchfork who was born and educated in Sheffield and who later served as the Commanding Officer of RAF Finningley, has rectified this omission by writing the detailed history of No.616 (South Yorkshire) Squadron.

Formed at Doncaster in 1938, the squadron maintained its deep roots in the County until it became a victim of defence cuts in 1957. In the intervening years, it played a unique role in the defence of our country, not least during the dark days of the Battle of Britain. It went on to carve a unique place in the history of the Royal Air Force by becoming the first and only Allied squadron to operate jets during the Second World War.

In post-war years, the squadron returned to its native South Yorkshire and local people again responded to the call for volunteers to serve. They helped preserve the peace during the Cold War and, in doing so, added to the unique history of No.616. The close links with the county were reinforced when the squadron was granted the Freedom of Entry into the County Borough of Doncaster.

Sadly, the squadron is no more but its proud heritage, and the gallant deeds of those men who served on 'South Yorkshire's Own', live on in the memory of the few survivors. But, one day, they too will fade from our consciousness. However, through the pages of this detailed and emotive history, their inspiring deeds will live on and future generations will, I am sure, feel a great sense of pride and admiration for those who served on No.616 (South Yorkshire) Squadron.

A splendid chapter provides a gripping account of the pivotal days of the Battle of Britain, and reminds us of the eternal debt we owe to those young men who wore their courage so lightly.

As a young boy I was taken to Battle of Britain Days at Finningley and also spent three years at Ranby House School to the noisy accompaniment of the Meteors taking off and landing at the airfield across the valley, so I feel a small part of the book. Now, as the Lord Lieutenant of this great county, I am delighted to have been given the opportunity to write these few words and to pay my respects to the courage of those who wrote a glorious chapter in South Yorkshire's history.

ACKNOWLEDGEMENTS

My interest in 616 (South Yorkshire) Squadron was stimulated when I was a boy and often cycled from my home in Sheffield to watch the Meteors flying from RAF Finningley at weekends. I started to collect material relating to the squadron, and I was privileged to meet many of the veterans when I commanded the very same airfield thirty years later. The result is that many of those who have given me valuable assistance and advice are, sadly, no longer with us.

I want to thank David Moody, the Lord Lieutenant of South Yorkshire, for his eloquent foreword. As the senior representative in the county, which provided a rich recruiting area for men to fly and service the squadron's aircraft, there can be no one better qualified to introduce the book and I am most grateful to him.

Before they passed away, 'Buck' Casson, Mike Cooper, Air Vice-Marshal Johnnie Johnson and Sid Woodacre gave me a great deal of material and photographs, which have proved invaluable. I am very grateful to Mrs Dorfy Casson for giving me access to Buck's papers and diaries, and also to Mrs Kitty Cooper for allowing me to quote from Mike's published papers and allowing me to use his photographs. Brian Mabbett told me about the brother he lost in July 1941 and gave me some photographs, which I am very pleased to have been able to include here. Neil Crabtree added details about his father's evasion and kindly lent me some photographs, which appear in the book.

Other squadron veterans have been very helpful and I thank William Abel, Dennis Barry, the late Ken Bown, Eric Brown, the late Sir Hugh 'Cocky' Dundas, Bob George, the late Eric King, Bob Large, Sid Little, Harry Mason and William Walker, the latter being the squadron's last surviving Battle of Britain pilot. I am also grateful to Dilip Sarkar for allowing me to use some quotes from his book *Bader's Tangmere Spitfires* (1996). I want to acknowledge the help given by an old friend, Ken Delve, who joined me in 1990, when we were both serving at RAF Finningley, in producing a short history of the squadron, *South Yorkshire's Own*, to commemorate the 50th Anniversary of the Battle of Britain. Mark Turner, secretary of the 616 Squadron Association, has been most helpful.

The Head of the Air Historical Branch, Sebastian Cox, and his excellent staff have given me a great deal of assistance, none more so than Graham Day. The staffs of the National Archives have been most helpful, and I am also indebted to colleagues Paul Baillie, Peter

Green, Jim Routledge, Andy Thomas and Group Captain Alan Tolhurst for their help and advice.

At The History Press I would like to thank Amy Rigg, Emily Locke and James Beer for all their help in bringing this project to fruition.

CHAPTER ONE

FORMATION AND BUILD UP

No.616 (South Yorkshire) Squadron, Royal Auxiliary Air Force.

From the earliest days of the Royal Air Force, its visionary and farsighted Chief of the Air Staff, Air Chief Marshal Sir Hugh Trenchard, appreciated the need for a reserve Air Force, which he believed should be organised on a territorial basis. Provision for such an Air Force Reserve and Auxiliary Air Force had been made in the Air Force Constitution Act of 1917 but it was not until 1924 that a draft Bill was to become law.

The then Secretary of State for Air, Sir Samuel Hoare (later Viscount Templewood), was a strong supporter of the Auxiliary Air Force. Many years later he was to pay this tribute:

Trenchard envisaged the Auxiliaries as a corps d'elite composed of the kind of young men who earlier would have been interested in horses, but who now wished to serve their country in machines. He conceived the new mechanical yeomanry with its aeroplanes based on the great centres of industry. Esprit de corps was to be the dominating force in the squadrons and each, therefore, was to have a well-equipped headquarters, mess, and distinctive life of its own. Social meetings were to be encouraged and on no account was any squadron to be regarded as a reserve for filling up regular units. The experiment was successful from the beginning. The forebodings of the doubters and critics were soon proved groundless. So, far from the non-regular units damaging the reputation of the regular squadrons they actually added some of the most glorious pages to the history of the Royal Air Force during the Second World War.

Initially, it was planned to form twenty auxiliary squadrons to be raised and maintained by the County Territorial Association and manned by locally recruited non-regular personnel, with only a small cadre of regulars as permanent staff and a non-regular commanding officer. In the event, with the storm clouds of war gathering over Europe, only sixteen squadrons were formed. The second last of these came into existence at Doncaster Airport on 1 November 1938, when Squadron Leader the Earl of Lincoln (later the Duke of

Squadron officers in 1939. *Standing, left to right:* Bell, Smith, Winn, Grimshaw, Dundas, Holden, Kellett, Wilson, Earl of Lincoln, Wood, Glover, Moberly, Hatchwell, Brewster, Casson, Roberts. *Front row:* Hellyer, St Aubyn, Murray, Graydon.

Second intake of ground crew arrive at Ellers Road, Doncaster.

Newcastle), was appointed to form No.616 (South Yorkshire) Auxiliary Air Force Squadron under Bomber Command.

Joining at the same time were Pilot Officers G.E. Moberly, from 609 Squadron, and E.F. St Aubyn, from 503 Squadron, and two regular officers, Flight Lieutenant D.S. Radford, to be the squadron's adjutant and flying instructor, and Flight Lieutenant H.M. Pim MC as the equipment officer. An advance party of two Senior NCOs (SNCO) and nineteen airmen also joined to be followed, on 10 November, by the main party of six Senior NCOs and twenty airmen. Intended initially as a light bomber squadron, the first aircraft, six Hawker Hinds, two Avro Tutors and two Avro 504Ns, arrived on the same day. Within five days, 616 had been transferred to Fighter Command and by early December, flying training and a major recruiting drive in the South Yorkshire area had commenced.

By the end of the month, Flying Officer the Honourable C.J.F. Winn joined as the administration officer and Flying Officer J.N. Glover, a regular officer, was posted in. The CO briefed the local press on the launch of a recruiting campaign and this had immediate results. The first twenty-two applicants were interviewed two days later and seven were accepted with others placed on a waiting list. Over the next ten days, a further sixty-four applicants were interviewed in addition to others who had applied for a commission. By Christmas, the Earl of Lincoln, George Moberly and 'Teddy' St Aubyn had started flying training.

The first thirty-three auxiliary airmen were attested on 21 January 1939, and they commenced their training immediately. Others followed during the month and another large intake, also of thirty-three, arrived on 19 February. With the exception of one or two posts, this completed the initial build up of the squadron.

The change to fighter status came into effect at the end of January with the departure of the Hinds and the arrival of Gloster Gauntlet fighters. Despite its antiquated appearance and very poor performance, the Gauntlet was not an old aircraft, having entered RAF service in 1935. Flying Officer R.D. Hellyer, another regular officer, arrived at the end of February, and Flight Lieutenant R.G. Kellett, an experienced fighter pilot, joined the South Yorkshire Squadron to assist in the conversion program.

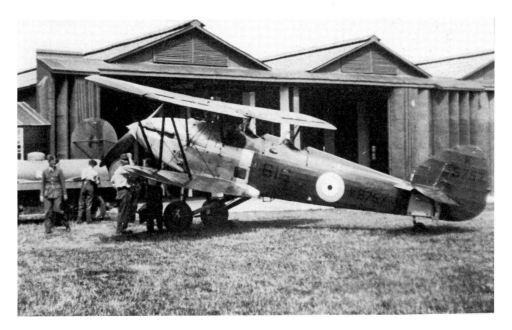

Hawker Hind (K 6757) at Doncaster.

Gloster Gauntlets at Doncaster, 1939.

Training continued and the first of the local auxiliary pilots, Mr Ken Holden, started his flying training on 16 March, achieving his first solo flight ten days later. With Messrs. J. Brewster, H.S.L. Dundas. R. Roberts and L.H. Casson, he had been one of the first auxiliary volunteers. His four friends were soon to solo on the Avro Tutor and three were to remain on 616 and serve with great distinction.

By the end of April, the CO, the Earl of Lincoln, was awarded his pilot's flying badge, and Ken Holden was appointed to a commission in the Royal Auxiliary Air Force. A new arrival from 19 Squadron, Pilot Officer R. Marples, would become one of the squadron's long-serving and leading pilots. On 20 May, the 23rd WAAF Company was affiliated to 616 Squadron under its Commandant Mrs Woodhead.

On 20 May, Empire Air Day was held at Doncaster under the direction of the civil authorities. All auxiliary officers and airmen were present, and Dudley Radford, John Glover and Dick Hellyer put on a flying display. The following day, another large intake of thirty-two airmen were attested and placed under training. To speed the training of pilots, and give experience with a modern monoplane type, two solo and two dual Fairey Battles were taken on strength at the end of the month.

The first significant operational milestone in the squadron's short existence came with the formation, on 10 June, of the Service Flight comprising of the Commanding Officer, Flight Lieutenant A. Wilson, Flying Officer R.D. Hellyer and Pilot Officers Teddy St Aubyn and George Moberly, the latter two having just been awarded their pilot's flying badge. At this stage, the squadron had six Gauntlets and the four Fairey Battles. Meanwhile, the training of the new pilots continued with Pilot Officer T.B. Murray receiving his commission by the end of June.

At this time the squadron was honoured when the Marquis of Titchfield MP (later the Duke of Portland) accepted the appointment as Honorary Air Commodore. Throughout

Avro Tutor trainer at Doncaster.

its existence, the Marquis was to show the keenest interest in the squadron's activities and welfare, including numerous visits, and his support was greatly appreciated.

On 23 July, John Brewster, 'Buck' Casson and 'Cocky' Dundas were commissioned as acting pilot officers. Casson was known as 'Buck' before joining 616, but the West Yorkshireman, Dundas, inherited his nickname from one of the more senior members of the squadron who addressed him as 'Cocky'. When he enquired why, the reply came, 'I couldn't remember your name and you look like a bloody great Rhode Island Red'! The name stuck, and he was known as 'Cocky' throughout his RAF career.

Summer camp at an operational flying station was an annual event for all Auxiliary Air Force squadrons. This allowed for intensive training and squadron work-ups. For 616 the first such deployment came in August 1939 when the squadron deployed to RAF Manston in Kent during the second week of August. At 15.00 on 23 August, the squadron received a signal ordering the embodiment of the Auxiliary Air Force and the squadron immediately returned to Doncaster to take up their war station. At 22.30 on the 25th, a signal was sent to the Air Ministry, Fighter Command and No.12 Group confirming that embodiment had been completed. Leading Aircraftman Max Williams of Doncaster, one of the first volunteers to join 616, summed up the moment: 'We went on two weeks' summer camp in Kent just before the war broke out and came home six-and-a-half years later.'

The squadron said goodbye to Dudley Radford, who was promoted and left to take command of a front-line squadron. Within the year he was awarded the DFC.

On 18 September, Squadron Leader W. Bieseigal assumed command of 616, and Acting Flight Lieutenant D.F. Gillam AFC, Flying Officer R. Miller and Pilot Officers H.K. Laycock, D.S. Smith and E.W.S. Scott were posted in to make up the operational strength. Within a month, the squadron had moved to the operational flying station at Leconfield in East Yorkshire, and on 30 October the first three Spitfire Mk 1s had been delivered. On

Spitfire I (L 1055) at readiness at Leconfield in April 1940.

14 November, eleven more Spitfires were transferred from 66 Squadron at Kemble, and training commenced in earnest.

Operational flying training for 616 Squadron, with its new Spitfires, commenced in December with air interception exercises, under the control of the nearby Sector Control Centre at RAF Church Fenton. Over the coming months, many operational sorties would be flown under the control of Church Fenton, so it was essential that the pilots and controllers became familiar with each other's operations. Gunnery practice took place regularly at RAF Acklington on the Northumberland coast, and at the end of the month eleven aircraft fired against sea markers. Twenty-seven thousand rounds of ammunition were fired. 'Considerable improvement' was noted, compared with the practises carried out earlier in the month.

As the New Year arrived, the squadron had twenty-three pilots on strength, of which four were sergeants. 'A' Flight was declared operational, and the squadron's first war patrol was flown on 11 January. During the month 616 flew many patrols escorting convoys along the North Sea coast, and on one such sortie the pilots had their first experience of the Germans jamming our aircraft's radio frequencies. By mid-February the whole squadron was declared fully operational as a day fighter squadron. At this time, the squadron's code letters were 'QJ', also adopted by 92 Squadron in an administration oversight which caused considerable confusion. No.616 Squadron retained 'QJ' codes until June 1941 when 'YQ' was allocated, thus preventing any further confusion.

On 21 February Church Fenton Operations scrambled Blue Section at 09.25 to escort a south-bound convoy off Scarborough. Flight Lieutenant Tony Wilson was leading the section and, once over the coast, he descended to low level to locate the convoy in the poor visibility. He was never seen again, and the squadron lost an excellent flight commander and pilot. When taking off on the same sortie, Flying Officer J.S. Bell collided with a Magister training aircraft. His aircraft was damaged and unfortunately the Magister pilot was killed. Flight Lieutenant Denys Gillam succeeded Tony Wilson in command of 'B' Flight.

Throughout February the weather was very severe with heavy falls of snow and for three weeks a large labour force of airmen armed with shovels had fought valiantly to keep the airfield open for flying, but the sudden thaw that followed made the ground so soft that the squadron had to detach to nearby RAF Catfoss for two weeks. The weather was not the only frustrating feature of the month's activities. Despite many scrambles, the squadron failed to make contact with the enemy as few raiders penetrated the squadron's sector, and those that did made skilful use of the cloud, thus denying the pilots the opportunity to attack. March and April proved to be equally frustrating with continuous poor weather and very few contacts with the enemy. Convoy patrols continued and the squadron arranged numerous practice interception sorties with the Whitley bomber squadron based at nearby RAF Driffield, and these exercises were to prove invaluable to both squadrons in the coming days.

Following the bad weather of January and February, the pilots had little opportunity to remain proficient at night, so a Master aircraft was flown to Leconfield to give them some dual night flying practice before continuing on the Spitfire. Lack of night flying eventually became so critical that a Harvard from the Instrument Flying School had to be loaned to the squadron.

On 1 May Squadron Leader W.K. Beisiegel was posted to the Staff College and he handed over command to Flight Lieutenant M. Robinson of 602 Squadron, who was immediately promoted to squadron leader. The 'Phony War' continued and the squadron had to be content with practising fighter tactics, formation flying and night flying. According to the squadron's operations log, the weather during this period was good since it was irreverently described as 'Group Captain's weather, no cloud, and visibility 10 miles'. However, the steady routine of the previous months changed suddenly on the dawn of 10 May when German forces invaded the Low Countries. All sections, usually twelve pilots, came to readiness at first light, and this became the routine for each following day. On 15 May, Ron Kellett, who had joined in the earliest days, left to join 249 Squadron as a flight commander. He fought with distinction throughout the Battle of Britain and was later awarded the DSO and DFC. Dick Hellyer replaced him in command of 'A' Flight.

In the early hours of 25 May the Sector Operations at Church Fenton asked the squadron to scramble an aircraft, despite the very poor weather, so the commanding officer took off to intercept a bomber that had been seen in the Humber area, but, due to the extensive cloud and poor visibility, he was unable to make contact. This was the first operational activity for some time but, with the German Armies sweeping through North West Europe, the whole squadron was soon to be in action.

CHAPTER TWO

BATTLE OF FRANCE

Throughout May the British Expeditionary Force (BEF), together with the Advanced Air Striking Force, had steadily retreated through Belgium and Northern France under the relentless 'blitzkrieg' of the German forces. By 14 May the German spearheads had captured Boulogne and arrived at the gates of Calais, cutting off the BEF from the main French army. The RAF was outnumbered, and without an adequate warning and control system they suffered crippling losses. The Commander-in-Chief of Fighter Command, Air Marshal Sir Hugh Dowding, could see that if squadrons continued to be sent to France as reinforcements then Fighter Command would cease to exist by the end of July, and Britain would stand undefended. On the following day Dowding wrote his famous and historic letter to the Under Secretary of State at the Air Ministry, outlining the gravity of the situation should further squadrons be transferred from the Home Defence Force to France. The cabinet approved a reduced flow of squadrons from Britain to France, but it was not until the 19th that Churchill decided that no further squadrons should be transferred. In fact, by the 21st all RAF fighter squadrons had been withdrawn from France because of the imminent collapse. In eleven days, the RAF had lost almost twenty-five per cent of its fighter force.

At the beginning of the final withdrawal of the Allied Armies and evacuation from Dunkirk, the Air Ministry ordered continuous weak fighter patrols throughout the eighteen hours of daylight. Not unexpectedly, this resulted in the RAF squadrons suffering heavy casualties for small successes in combat. After strong representation to higher authority, 11 Group was permitted to employ offensive patrols of two-squadron strength, leaving a few hours of daylight in which there were no patrols on the line. This resulted in fewer casualties to our fighters and a marked increase in the number of successes in combat. When the enemy formations were of thirty to sixty bombers, closely escorted by formations of fifteen to thirty fighters, permission was obtained to employ offensive sweeps by four squadrons working in two pairs. Whenever possible, Spitfires provided the high-level cover with the low-level provided by either Hurricanes, or a mix of Hurricanes and Defiants. This employment was most successful in reducing our casualties and increasing the number of enemy aircraft shot down.

On 26 May the Dunkirk evacuation began and fighters of 11 Group gave continuous air cover whenever the weather allowed. On the first day of the evacuation, 616 was ordered to move to Rochford airfield, near Southend, to relieve 74 Squadron, and to join the Hornchurch Wing with 19 and 65 Squadrons. Eighteen Spitfires arrived at Rochford the next day, and in the late evening twelve aircraft, led by the squadron commander, were airborne to join the rest of the Wing patrolling between Dunkirk and Gravelines, but no contact was made with the enemy. The pilots on this first major sortie of the war for 616 were the CO, Gillam, Hellyer, Moberly, Holden, D.S. Smith, Laycock, Bell, Scott, Dundas, St Aubyn and Flight Sergeant Burnard.

No.616 was ordered to patrol with 19 and 65 Squadrons over the Dunkirk beaches early on the morning of 28 May. Squadron Leader D. Cooke, the Commanding Officer of 65 Squadron, led the Wing. On reaching the patrol line, some Spitfires were seen attacking two unidentified aircraft (which turned out to be Fleet Air Arm Skuas), and in positioning to identify them the squadron became separated from the main formation. Almost immediately, thirty Messerschmitt Me 109s attacked Red and Green sections. Squadron Leader Robinson's aircraft was hit and severely disabled and he was just able to make the English coast and crash-land at RAF Manston. Ken Holden, flying as Red 4, was attacked and immediately pulled his aircraft into a high-G turn, which put him on the tail of a Me 109. Firing a 10-degree deflection burst he hit the enemy, which belched thick black smoke before pitching up violently and spinning out of control over Dunkirk. In the meantime George Moberly had put his Green section into line astern, and engaged emergency boost to gain height to join the engagement with Red Section. A Me 109 slanted across his nose and he fired at a range of 200 yards. The enemies' starboard wing broke off immediately. He was forced to break off his attack as other Me 109s began closing in on him. Scott (Green 2) followed his leader into the attack, and fired a short burst at another Me 109 which rolled on to its back with blue smoke pouring from the port wing. He was unable to follow the enemy down as he was hit by cannon fire and had to dive away to escape. In the engagement, Sergeant M. Ridley was wounded in the forehead, but managed to land his badly damaged Spitfire safely. Dick Hellyer failed to return from this sortie. Happily he returned twenty-four hours later having crash-landed on the beach at Dunkirk and hitch-hiked back to England by boat.

For several days the squadron continued to patrol over the troops on the beaches without making contact with the enemy. On 1 June the squadron was ordered to patrol over the Dunkirk beaches from 05.00 to 06.15, to protect the ships evacuating troops from the port. Ten aircraft were airborne at 04.02, and approaching the coast. Red Section, led by the CO, saw a Dornier 17 attacking shipping while several Me 109s provided air cover. Red section dived in to attack, but the thick layer of cloud, allied to poor visibility, aided the enemy's escape, but not before they had been briefly engaged. The CO fired three bursts at a Me 109 before it escaped into cloud, and St Aubyn fired at another before it was also lost in cloud. As he approached Dunkirk at 2,000 feet, Ken Holden saw two Me 109s circling warships, so he gave chase to one firing a long burst into it. Small flames came from the engine and it rolled onto its back, diving into cloud. Joining up with another squadron, attacking some Junkers 88s, he saw a lone Me 109, which took no avoiding action as he approached. After two bursts, the enemy caught fire and ditched in the sea. Holden used so much fuel in his dogfight that he had to force land at Rochester with his tanks empty. Jack Bell became separated from the rest of the section but found and attacked eight Me 109s. He managed to shoot one down before he too was forced down on the sea. Fortunately he was picked up by the Royal Navy. His combat report gives a graphic account of the action and his rescue:

I was flying in the box of the leading section (Red 4) of No.616 Squadron on Offensive Patrol over Dunkirk. When approaching Dunkirk we found 2-4 Me 109s (and, I have since learnt, one Do 17) attacking a ship. The e/a were machine-gunning it. As one was directly below me, I pulled round in a very tight turn to get on its tail. Unfortunately the turn was too rough, and caused my engine to lose all power and refuse to respond to the throttle. I thought at the time that a piece of AA fire must have hit my engine, so had opened the hood in order to bail out, when the engine came on again. I flew round looking for my squadron, but was unable to find it before the other two squadrons on patrol appeared in formation above me. I joined up with them and flew alongside to see if my leader was with them. When nearing the front of the formation I saw eight Me 109's in line astern machine-gunning a ship. I pointed downwards in the hope that someone in the formation would see them also, and then dived on the last e/a with my emergency boost. As I got on to his tail I saw that the leading e/a were coming round for a second attack on the ship. The leader had clearly seen me, so I looked around for the Spitfires but saw them wheeling away in the other direction. I closed in firing short bursts until smoke poured from the aircraft, the wings appeared to flap and it dived to the sea. During the earlier part of the attack I noticed occasional white puffs from the port side of the fuselage, and wondered whether this was a canon in the root of the wing or the tail plane. If it was I think the shots must have passed under me. I then had to execute a series of steep turns, with short intervals straight and level when I turned to steer west, but my compass never had time to settle down. I found that I could turn inside the Me 109 very easily, at an IAS of 140-180mph, but that he caught me up each time I flew straight. One aircraft appeared to use all its ammunition as he went away, but another one immediately started. I continued the same tactics but was caught after about four turns just as I was going into another turn. There was quite a loud explosion in the bottom of my engine, which stopped. Yellow flames appeared from the exhausts and there was a smell of fumes. I completed the turn and started gliding towards a ship; as my height was only 500 feet I did not care to bail out. I undid my straps, oxygen tube and R/T plug before hitting the water. I did not lower my flaps. Immediately on touching down my nose dipped and I was thrown forward. I struggled out under water keeping my parachute on. I came to the surface and found the tail plane still floating, so I pulled myself under this to hide in case I was fired on. The e/a did in fact fire about 10 more rounds and then turned away. I doubt if he had any ammunition left. I then swam to the ship, which was, I think, about 2 miles away, by the beach, taking on men from the BEF. While swimming I saw one Me 109 crash on the sand dunes. Me 109s were machine-gunning the beach many times, also the few boats going between the shore and the ships. I was finally picked up about 300 yards from the ship by a ship's pram, manned by a rating and a private who had volunteered to come out; this was the last remaining small boat on the ship, which was HM Sloop *Halcyon*. As I was taken onboard we started off for Dunkirk harbour. We were in the harbour for some time, perhaps forty-five minutes. All this time Ju 87s were dive-bombing ships in the harbour and at the entrance. We were firing with 4" guns, Lewis guns and Bren guns, all the time, while those of us who could find serviceable rifles, took pot shots with them. We could also see 109s machine-gunning the beach from time to time, and were disappointed to observe our own fighters flying in neat formation a few miles out to sea. Once clear of the harbour we saw fighter patrols fairly frequently and were only bombed once, by a Ju 88, which dropped a salvo of four bombs to starboard and then returned and dropped another salvo of eight to port, they did not appear to be very big bombs. This machine bombed us from a height of about 4,000 feet, and appeared to do a short dive from 5,000 down to 4,000 feet instead of a run up. Results were fairly accurate. The Ju 87s, which attacked the harbour, appeared in threes and dived down in line astern from 4,000 feet. They released their bombs and started to pull out at about 1,000 feet. All the attacks that I saw commencing started the dive with a turn to port. I landed at Dover at about 13.30. Members of the ship's crew and BEF told me that they had seen a Me 109 crash into the sea shortly before I crashed, and also an English fighter crash on the sand dunes – this latter was, I think, actually the Me 109 which I myself saw.

Leading the second sortie of the day, Denys Gillam took off with eight other aircraft, at 08.25, to patrol between Dunkirk and Furnes, with 19, 41 and 222 Squadrons. The squadron set up a patrol just below the cloud base at 3,500 feet, and soon intercepted a number of unescorted bombers. Gillam took his section amongst the bombers, which were bombing the evacuation ships, and a number of the enemy were severely damaged. George Moberly had initially kept his section clear; then he saw more bombers appearing above. Applying full boost he climbed steeply towards a Junkers 88, which immediately opened fire on him. Rapidly overhauling the enemy, he gave it a five-second burst, silencing the rear gunner. As he closed to 50 yards he saw the rudder and elevators fall from the aircraft, which then dived straight into the sea. Sergeant P. Copeland attacked a number of the enemy, and scored hits on a Heinkel 111, which stalled and exploded. Although given as a 'probable', it is very doubtful that this aircraft could have reached its base. Miller attacked and hit two Junkers 88s, forcing them to jettison their load of bombs. Marples and Laycock were credited with damaging a Heinkel 111 each, and D.S. Smith damaged a Junkers 88.

The Squadron launched a dawn patrol over the beaches on 2 June, but no contact was made with the enemy. There was a heavy ground mist in the early morning of the 3rd and it was thought that it might not be possible to carry out a patrol, but instructions were received to do so if 'humanly possible'. The CO led ten aircraft and successfully carried out the patrol. On the following morning the same conditions prevailed, but once again the importance of carrying out the early morning patrol was stressed. Nine aircraft took-off at 04.17 to patrol Dunkirk, but Pilot Officer E.W.S. Scott lost his life on take-off when he crashed due to the poor weather conditions. The remaining aircraft carried out the patrol, but had to divert to RAF Tangmere because of a layer of fog at Rochford. The Air Officer Commanding No.11 Group, Air Vice Marshal Keith Park, sent a signal of congratulation for the squadron's determined patrolling of 3 and 4 June despite the very poor visibility. By the 6th the historic evacuation of Dunkirk was complete and the squadron returned to Leconfield. The squadron had claimed its first 'kills', but it had also been bloodied in battle, with the loss of one pilot and three aircraft. Denys Gillam summed up the squadron's performance:

Most of the 616 Squadron sorties were in close support to the Army – up and down the beach at 1,000 to 2,000 feet. Consequently, we couldn't intercept but got involved only as the Germans dived away. Compared to later campaigns it was not a great occasion for us, but at the time we felt we had been really blooded.

Denys Gillam.

The Battle of France was over, but it was only a matter of time before the Battle of Britain would start. In the meantime the lull in activity gave the Commander-in-Chief precious time to reinforce his depleted squadrons. Pilot Officer W.L.B. Walker and Sergeants J.P. Walsh, P.T. Wareing and T.E. Westmoreland joined the squadron direct from flying training schools. During this period the squadron saw little activity until Jack Bell intercepted a lone Heinkel 111 as he was patrolling between base and Hull at 10,000 feet. On seeing the attacking Spitfire, the enemy dived to 200 feet and, after a short burst from Bell's guns, the bomber jettisoned its bombs and turned for home with smoke pouring from its tail.

In the early part of the war, single-seat fighter aircraft were not equipped to fight at night but, with very few radar-equipped Blenheims available, it was sometimes necessary to scramble lone Spitfires. Night fighting successfully was both demanding and difficult, and it required the utmost co-operation between the pilot, sector controller and the searchlight batteries. The recently arrived William Walker summed up the feelings of most of his fellow Spitfire pilots when, many years later, he said: 'Flying a Spitfire at night was the most hair-raising thing I did in the war. It could be quite terrifying. You were watching your instruments, exhausts were red hot and glowing and the chances of seeing anything at night were virtually nil.'

When Donald Smith was scrambled, just after midnight on 26 June, he arrived over Hull as the searchlights were illuminating a Heinkel 111. He attacked twice from below, closing to less than 100 yards, and silencing the gunner on his second pass. On his third attack the bomber banked violently, almost causing a collision. The Heinkel crashed shortly afterwards. Smith remarked that 'the searchlights revealed the enemy magnificently'. The whole interception was an excellent example of perfect co-ordination and skilful flying. Three nights later Roy Marples was scrambled at 00.50 to patrol between Pickering and Driffield at 10,000 feet. He had just started an orbit when the Withernsea searchlight illuminated an enemy aircraft at 15,000 feet. Marples attacked from dead astern, and his first burst brought an immediate response from the enemy gunner. A second burst silenced him, thick smoke obscured the bomber, and it was last seen in a shallow dive with its engines on fire. Later that night the crew of a Heinkel 111 were picked up off the coast, but said a twin-engine aircraft shot them down, so Marples could only claim a 'probable'. This was one of the very few successful night interceptions by Spitfires and was a magnificent performance by Marples. Later the same night, Ken Holden was scrambled and he chased two enemy aircraft north of Catterick, but was unable to engage.

CHAPTER THREE

BATTLE OF BRITAIN

At the outset of the greatest air battle in history, it is worth recalling the aim of Hitler's War Directive No.16. The aim was, 'To eliminate Great Britain as a base from which the war against Germany can be fought. If necessary the island will be occupied.'

In order to achieve this aim, Hitler ordered that the main preparation to be undertaken in order to make an invasion in England possible should be, 'The elimination of the English Air Force…'

The Luftwaffe had never known defeat, so Reichsmarschall Herman Goering, the Commander-in-Chief, assured the Fuhrer that this could easily be achieved.

It is generally accepted that the Battle of Britain commenced on 10 July and finished on 31 October, with the heaviest fighting occurring between 8 August and 21 September. The month of July could be considered as a month of skirmishes, with attacks on British coastal convoys, and a steady build up in activity as the month progressed, until the major assaults of August and September. As the Battle developed, 616 was to become heavily involved at the very front of the battle area.

At the beginning of July, 616 Squadron, with a pilot strength of twenty, and equipped with fifteen Spitfire Mk 1s, was still based at RAF Leconfield in East Yorkshire, and formed part of 12 Group of Fighter Command.

Early in the morning of 1 July, the squadron was preparing for a day of routine training, typical of all fighter squadrons, and to include air tactics, cine-gun attacks and formation flying. Just after 09.00 three pilots of Yellow Section were on an air combat training flight, with Bob Miller leading two of the new pilots, Pilot Officers R.A. Smith and Bill Walker, on a 'tail chasing' tactics demonstration, when the Sector Controller warned them to look out for an enemy raider in their area. Contact was made with a Dornier 17 bomber flying at 20,000 feet, and Miller closed in to attack, firing a long burst at the enemy with Smith following with another short burst. Walker then closed in and set himself up astern of the bomber for a close-range attack, but on firing his guns there was no response and he realised that they hadn't been loaded – his aircraft had been configured for a cine-gun practise sortie – so the Dornier escaped. It immediately became squadron policy to load all aircraft guns irrespective of the type of sortie!

'B' Flight ground crew at Leconfield, August 1940.

During the afternoon Miller was airborne again, this time in company with Jack Bell and John Brewster, when they were directed to a Heinkel 111, last seen over Hull and going out to sea. The fighters were unable to close in, but whilst returning saw another Heinkel 111, which they intercepted. Miller opened the attack, damaging the aircraft and silencing the rear gunner. Brewster followed and his first attack set the port engine on fire, so he transferred his fire to the starboard engine. As he closed to 200 yards his windscreen was covered in engine oil from the enemy bomber, which started emitting thick black smoke. He fired three bursts and saw more bits break off, before the burning Heinkel dived into the sea.

During 3 July the Luftwaffe made numerous light attacks on coastal targets, including some by aircraft of Luftflotte 5, based in Scandinavia. Green Section of 616 was scrambled at 09.00 to intercept a raider approaching the Yorkshire coast. George Moberly, 'Cocky' Dundas and Flight Sergeant F.P. Burnard encountered a Dornier 17 at 4,500 feet. All three aircraft made two passes each, and the aircraft crashed into the sea, but not before Dundas' aircraft had been hit in the wing. However, this did not prevent him joining Burnard in engaging a second Dornier, which, after being hit and damaged, managed to escape into cloud.

Throughout July, the Luftwaffe continued to attack coastal targets and to harass our convoys. The squadron was scrambled regularly and spent many hours patrolling over the East Coast convoys, but the enemy restricted most of its attacks to the south of England. The weather was particularly inclement for the time of the year. Early in the month, Yellow Section was scrambled to 20,000 feet, but, because of very thick cloud, they were forced to split up. Sergeant Copeland's main instruments failed, and he became disorientated. He wisely decided to bale out, but he could not open his cockpit hood so he had no choice but to remain with his aircraft. Somehow he managed to regain control of his Spitfire and eventually made a successful landing at Kirton in Lindsay airfield, very shaken but safe.

July had been a month of constant probing by the Luftwaffe in an effort to discover weaknesses in Britain's defences. Although some were found, Dowding and his group commanders were able to plug them before they could be exploited. As the month came to an end, the weight of air attacks increased and, as the weather improved, there was every reason to think that the major onslaught would commence. Surprisingly there was no significant increase in attacks early in the month. It turned out that the Germans were merely finalising their plans for an all out air assault (Eagle Attack), prior to their invasion of England, planned for the middle of September (Operation Sealion).

Meanwhile, before the onslaught began, the squadron continued to carry out convoy patrols. On 1 August, Sergeant M. Ridley chased a Junkers 88 out to sea, getting in a good burst of 600 rounds and observing black smoke coming from the bomber. Ridley's aircraft was hit in the engine and radio by return fire, but not seriously damaged. Three days later tragedy struck. While carrying out dog fighting practise with Yellow Section, Sergeant John Walsh spun into the ground from 5,000 feet, and was killed. He is buried in Harrow Cemetery.

Together with the routine convoy patrols, the squadron continued to carry out training, and it was not uncommon for sections to be 'scrambled' in the air by the Sector Controllers to investigate raiders. On 6 August Red Section, led by the squadron commander, was vectored to an enemy aircraft flying at 20,000 feet. It turned out to be a Junkers 88, and, as Squadron Leader Robinson fired a long burst, the bomber started smoking. Sergeant Ridley then attacked, but before No.3, Dick Hellyer, could get a good burst in, the damaged Ju 88 dived into cloud. No losses were reported so it must be assumed that the aircraft managed to regain its base in Scandinavia or Holland. During the attack, all three Spitfires were hit by pieces of debris from the enemy, but all landed safely.

Many of the newer pilots at this time had very little night flying experience, so every opportunity was taken to practise. Shortly after taking off on the night of 7 August, Pilot Officer R.A. Smith crashed eight miles from the airfield and was killed. His aircraft appeared to get into a dive at about 1,200 feet, but the cause was never determined. A few days later he was buried with full military honours in the local churchyard. On the same evening, Sergeant T. Westmoreland crashed on landing and escaped unhurt, although his aircraft was severely damaged. A few days later, 'Buck' Casson hit an obstruction on take-off and damaged his undercarriage. He had to make an immediate crash landing, during which his aircraft was destroyed. Fortunately he was unhurt. Needless to say, the loss of these aircraft in training accidents could be

Teddy St Aubyn poses with his aircraft after the mishaps of the previous night's flying.

ill-afforded. Indeed, in the first two weeks of August, Fighter Command had no less than twenty-one aircraft destroyed and fourteen severely damaged in training accidents. However, it must be remembered that these young pilots were having to be rushed to man the fighter squadrons, and some had as little as ten hours on their aircraft type. Their subsequent deeds speak for themselves. They may have lacked experience, but they more than compensated with raw courage.

The second week of August saw an increased tempo of Luftwaffe activity, and many military historians consider 8 August as the opening day of the Battle of Britain. As a prelude to the invasion, the German High Commander's aim was to destroy the Royal Air Force, but their strategy never identified the specific aim of destroying all the elements of Fighter Command first, in order to gain air superiority. Instead, there were many objectives, including the bombing of ports, coastal shipping and other RAF units. Having selected the right aim, they failed to achieve it, and to concentrate their numerical superiority to maximum effect. This critical failure of Goering's gave Dowding and his commanders just enough flexibility to use their dedicated, if limited, forces to their full potential. Furthermore, German intelligence had failed to fully appreciate the extent and capability of the fighter control system; radar sites and operation rooms that Dowding had established. This was to precipitate one of the greatest blunders of the war, when Hitler and Goering claimed that radar sites were too difficult to hit and transferred the Luftwaffe's attention to other targets.

Initially, convoys remained primary targets, but within a few days heavy attacks against radar sites and fighter airfields began in preparation for the German invasion. Following a very strenuous day on 12 August, Air Marshal Dowding realised that his hard-pressed squadrons in the south might need reinforcing, and he alerted five squadrons in the north to be ready to move south, amongst them 616.

The German's failure to launch 'Eagle Day' on the 12th caused frustration amongst the High Command, and Goering called his commanders together for discussions. The Luftwaffe had been badly mauled in the previous few days, and thus it was a surprise that they should launch such a massive attack on the 15th, without appearing to take note of the lessons learned. Perhaps the attendance of so many senior commanders at Goering's conference, allied to questionable intelligence, may offer an explanation.

The German plan was to synchronise attacks by Luftlotte 5, based in Norway and Denmark, against the north of England, with those mounted by the two air fleets based in northern France. In the past Luftlotte 5 had made only sporadic attacks in the north, but the strength of Fighter Command's retaliation and defence in the south in the preceding days of heavy fighting convinced the German intelligence staff that the north of England could only be lightly defended. Therefore, it was decided to attack the north in force and, because of the long range, without fighter escort.

Knowing that the German air fleets in Scandinavia had the range to mount heavy attacks against the industrial complexes in the north, Dowding had steadfastly resisted the temptation to base all his fighters in the south. Due to poor intelligence, the German High Command were unaware that there were a number of first-rate squadrons in the north, which were well rested and fighting fit after their endeavours over Dunkirk. By the end of the day, the General Commanding Luftflotte 5 was left in no doubt as to the vigilance of the northern CH radar stations, and the strength and ability of the fighter squadrons in the area.

The day started cloudy, which delayed the launch of the bombers in Norway and Denmark, but a ridge of high pressure was soon established over the whole of Britain, giving fine and warm weather. Massive raids were aimed at the fighter airfields in the south of England during the morning, but, as the controllers scanned the operations' tables for further build-ups after midday, it was to the north that the Battle moved.

Unknown to the German planners, a large and very important convoy was due to depart from Hull at midday, so all the East Coast radar stations were in a high state of readiness and vigilance. Taking off at 10.00 from their bases at Stavanger in Norway and Aalborg in Denmark, the German bombers had a two-hour flight to the British coast. Just after midday controllers at the East Coast radar sites started to detect two simultaneous heavy attacks in the north and north-east. Immediately, all fighter squadrons were brought to maximum readiness, amongst them 616 at Leconfield.

The Staxton Wold radar station, near Bridlington, plotted a raid of forty plus aimed directly at the fighter stations of Church Fenton and Leconfield. 616 was scrambled and ordered to patrol over Flamborough Head. The call came just as the two Flights were in the process of changing over the 'readiness' duty, so the whole squadron was able to scramble. Such was the spirit of the squadron that George Moberly, who was on a day's leave, on hearing the scramble, leapt into a spare Spitfire and roared off fifteen minutes behind his colleagues. Fourteen Spitfires scrambled, and for their first major battle the squadron's sections were:

'B' Flight pilots at Leconfield, August 1940. *Standing left to right:* Marples, Dundas, Laycock, Gillam (Flt Cdr), Murray, Casson, Wareing. *Front:* Westmoreland, Hopewell, Burnard.

Red: CO, Hellyer, D.S. Smith, Westmoreland.
Yellow: Bell, Brewster, Walker.
Blue: Gillam, Murray, Marples.
Green: Dundas, Casson, Hopewell, Moberly.

The squadron was vectored to patrol over Flamborough, and at 13.15 intercepted a formation of some fifty Junkers 88 bombers of *Kampf Geschwader 30* flying without escort from Aalborg in Denmark. Denys Gillam, leading 'B' Flight, was the first to spot the enemy at 19,000 feet, fifteen miles east of Bridlington, and he immediately led Blue Section into the attack. Squadron pilots reported that the enemy aircraft were flying in a very poor formation, with several stragglers. Seeing the Spitfires, the bombers split into numerous small formations, with some bombing Bridlington while others attacked the bomber airfield at Driffield, destroying ten Whitleys, whilst a number turned for home.

Roy Marples got the first burst in on a bomber and, as he broke away, Gillam took over and kept up a continuous fire. The Ju 88 dived to 6,000 feet where it jettisoned its bombs. Part of the tail broke away and the aircraft turned onto its back enveloped in flames, before crashing into the sea. Meanwhile, Marples, having pulled off from his first attack, immediately pursued another bomber in the formation, getting in two bursts before it entered cloud with one engine smoking. He then saw two other bombers north of Scarborough, and gave chase firing short bursts. One aircraft wheeled to port and dived to ground level, but Marples could only harass the bomber since he had run out of ammunition. Murray (Blue 2) saw two Ju 88s flying through broken cloud at 10,000 feet. They were in close formation, with one smoking badly. He fired three long bursts and a second or two after the last burst both bombers caught fire. He did not see them crash but it is most unlikely that they survived the attack.

Dundas, leading Green Section, saw Gillam lead his section into the attack and, after Marples had broken away, having severely damaged his second aircraft, he closed in and fired a three-second burst, setting both engines on fire. The enemy bomber crashed into the sea ten miles east of Flamborough. Each pilot was credited with a half aircraft destroyed. Casson (Green 2) had followed Dundas in, but being poorly placed, broke away to intercept a lone Ju 88 heading out to sea at 5,000 feet. After two quarter attacks, the enemy dived to 1,000 feet with the rear gunner keeping up a steady fire. Casson fired two more bursts, and the aircraft dived to sea level, at which point Dundas reappeared and, since Casson's ammunition was exhausted, took over the attack. By now there was no return fire, and the enemy was last seen severely damaged at very low level with smoke pouring from its port engine.

Red Section also attacked the main bomber force at 18,000 feet. The CO, Squadron Leader Robinson, damaged one bomber before he ran out of ammunition. Hellyer, with D.S. Smith in company, dived astern a Ju 88 and fired all his ammunition into it before Smith took up the attack, firing short bursts until the enemy suddenly dived steeply in to the sea.

By now, the bombers were completely split up, and a number of individual actions occurred. Hopewell picked out a lone Ju 88 heading out to sea at 9,000 feet, and attacked it, hitting both wings. The bomber took violent evasive action, turning inland. Hopewell continued to fire into the engines, and pieces started to break off. Shortly afterwards the aircraft crashed, three miles north-west of Bridlington. Westmoreland also attacked a lone Ju 88 heading back to Denmark, firing a two-second burst from 400 yards. On the second attack, the port engine caught fire and one of the crew baled out.

Finally, Moberly arrived on the scene. Having got airborne fifteen minutes behind the rest of the squadron, he had been listening on the radio, decided to make for Flamborough. Before arriving he saw a twin-engine aircraft well below him heading out to sea. He dived to 2,000 feet and identified a Ju 88 with smoke coming from an engine (probably the aircraft attacked by Westmoreland). He attacked two or three times before the enemies' starboard engine stopped, and shortly afterwards he saw it crash into the sea.

In a few minutes the squadron had claimed eight enemy destroyed and six seriously damaged for no loss. Post-war analysis suggests that some of these claims may have been shared with another squadron, but 616 seem justified in claiming five destroyed. Whatever the claims, Luftlotte 5 never again tried to attack the north and, as a result of their failure, many of their aircraft were transferred to France to reinforce Luftflotte 2. So ended a memorable day in the history of 616 Squadron; a day which came to be known throughout the Luftwaffe as 'Black Thursday', with seventy-five aircraft lost in combat over Britain. Bill Walker, who had flown as Yellow 3, summed up the feelings of most of the 616 pilots:

> There was never really time to be nervous. You knew what you had to do. I was utterly amazed. It was the first time I had seen such a large flight of aircraft. It was also the first time I had fired my guns in anger. I shot at three, so my log book says, went back and rearmed.

Despite their losses, there was no sign of the enemy reducing its attacks, and 18 August was to see some very heavy attacks on RAF airfields in the south and east of England. Losses amongst the RAF fighter squadrons were increasing, and it was apparent to Dowding that he would have to transfer fresh squadrons to the south. The following day orders came for 616 to move to RAF Kenley in Surrey, to share the defence of London against pre-invasion attacks.

Just after midday on 19 August, the squadron, led by the two flight commanders, Gillam and Hellyer, took off for Kenley. At lunchtime, an advance party of ground crew left by air. There followed two relatively quiet days, but the increased level of activity can be gathered by the message passed by operations and recorded in the squadron's operational diary. Pilots were reminded that whenever possible they must return after combat to their airfield of departure to re-arm and refuel at speed, to come to readiness for the next patrol in squadron strength. This was later amplified to tell pilots and ground crews that they must come to readiness 'in the shortest possible time after landing for combat'. Even the interrogation of pilots by intelligence was on no account to delay the return of a squadron to readiness.

At 18.45 on 22 August 616 was scrambled. Fourteen Spitfires took off and were immediately vectored to patrol over Hawkinge at 15,000 feet to intercept an incoming raid. Nothing was seen and the squadron turned towards Dover, but no sooner had they arrived there than twelve Me 109s bounced them and dived to attack Green Section. Almost immediately the 'tail-end Charlie' of the squadron formation, Dundas' aircraft, was hit, and he was wounded in the arms and legs. With his controls shot to bits and his aircraft on fire, he tried to bale out, but could not open the cockpit hood. He spun out of control at 12,000 feet, and finally managed to escape from his aircraft at 800 feet, sustaining further injuries on landing, which put him out of action for a month. The squadron operations' log noted that 'the aircraft was completely u/s'! Another Me 109 was attacking Green 3, so Sergeant Wareing dived onto the enemies' tail, following it in a steep dive to port. After being hit by a number of short bursts fired from 300 to 400 yards, the Me 109 levelled out and slowed down, allowing Wareing to fire another short burst which set the aircraft on fire. Blue Leader saw the action and observed the 109 going down in flames close to a burning Spitfire, which turned out to be that of Dundas.

The 24th was the first day of a crucial and critical phase of the Battle of Britain, which was to last until 6 September. The Luftwaffe's aim was to destroy Fighter Command by attacking the airfields in the south. Despite being scrambled three times on this hectic day, the squadron failed to make contact with the enemy. However, the same could not be said of the next day. After a quiet start to the day, twelve Spitfires of 616 were scrambled at 18.20, with five other squadrons, to intercept a heavy raid aimed towards the Kent airfields. Over Canterbury the squadron intercepted fifteen to twenty Dornier 17s flying at 17,000 feet, escorted by up to twenty Me 109s flying in a staggered line at 20,000 feet. The enemy fighters dived onto 616, breaking up the formation. A big dogfight ensued, in which a number of Me 109s were engaged and damaged, Moberly shooting one down and Bell attacking another, which was on the tail of a Spitfire, causing it to break away. He chased it out to sea where he eventually set the enemy on fire. It immediately dived into cloud; Bell could only claim a probable. Sergeant Ridley managed to disengage from the main dogfight with the Me 109s, and closed in on one of the bombers, shooting it down over the sea. However, the squadron paid dearly for its successes. Both Tom Westmoreland and Philip Wareing failed to return with Green Section, and it was soon confirmed that Westmoreland, whose parents lived in Huddersfield, had died in his Spitfire as it crashed near Canterbury. A few days later, the squadron learnt that Wareing had baled out over the Channel, been rescued by the Germans and made a prisoner of war. Two years later he made a brilliant escape from Oflag XXI at Schubin, and reached Sweden in January 1943. Shortly afterwards he was awarded the Distinguished Conduct Medal; an award rarely made to RAF personnel.

The pattern of daylight raids on the 26th was much the same as that of the previous day, only this time RAF Biggin Hill and 616's base at Kenley were singled out for attack. As the first major raid of the day was detected over the Channel, Air Vice Marshal Park scrambled some seventy fighters to intercept the bombers. 616 managed to scramble only seven aircraft, just after 11.00, to intercept two raids of forty plus bombers flying at 17,000 feet over Shoreham. They were too late to attack the Heinkels, so turned north, immediately running into almost 100 Me 109s, which attacked from 3,000 feet above them. Blue Section turned into a defensive circle whilst trying to gain height and await reinforcements. Before help could arrive on the scene, the enemy fighters pounced. Within minutes the Spitfires of St Aubyn, Marples and Sergeant Copeland had been hit and severely damaged, with all three pilots being wounded. Despite their injuries they all managed to crash-land in the Kent countryside without further injury, but all the aircraft were destroyed and none of the pilots recovered in time to take any further part in the Battle. Meanwhile, after a forty-minute delay on the ground, five Spitfires of 'A' Flight had scrambled to patrol Dungeness, and, as they climbed to gain height, they were caught unawares, and within seconds George Moberly and Sergeant Marmaduke Ridley had been shot down and killed. Walker and Bell were also shot down. Bell managed to crash-land at Beckesbourne, escaping unhurt. Bill Walker remembered the day well:

> I was allocated Spitfire R 6633 and was to fly in Yellow Section. It was very early when we were scrambled. I leapt on to the wing and was in the cockpit, parachute strapped on, within seconds. We flew in wide formation and had been airborne for about an hour when suddenly Me 109s appeared and bounced us. I banked sharply to port, towards an Me 109, when my Spitfire was raked with bullets from another behind me in my blind spot. The controls ceased to respond and a sudden pain in my leg indicated that I had been hit. Baling out seemed to be a sensible option.

Sergeant Marmaduke Ridley
(KIA; 26 August 1940).

I pulled back the hood and tried to stand but realized that I had not disconnected the radio chord and I had to take off my helmet. I was at 20,000 feet and pulled the ripcord immediately. There was a sudden jerk and I was on my way down. It seemed to take ages and I passed through some cloud and realized I was still over the Channel. I removed my heavy boots and inflated my Mae West as I landed in the sea. Even though I was nowhere near land, I had come down near a sandbank and I could see the mast of a wreck, which I swam towards and clambered out of the water. Amazingly, a fishing boat was nearby and, within half an hour, I was on my way to Ramsgate.

Bill Walker was taken to hospital and underwent an operation where a .303 bullet was removed from his ankle.

In the confusion of fighting only one 616 Squadron pilot managed to bring his gun sight to bear with any effect. Gillam chased a Me 109 that had attacked another Spitfire. Firing at his target from 11,000 feet down to 4,000 feet, he followed his victim through cloud, emerging on the other side to see it crash into the sea. After destroying the enemy aircraft he was attacked by a number of other fighters, but managed to escape.

Only five of the twelve Spitfires returned to Kenley, and in a few minutes the squadron had lost six pilots, two being killed. So ended a black day for 616. The loss of the two original pilots who had formed the squadron, George Moberly and Teddy St Aubyn, was a great blow to everyone in 616. St Aubyn, who was wounded and badly burned, made a good recovery, but was killed in action in a Mustang during May 1943, when returning across the English Channel at low level.

After two relatively quiet days, the squadron was back in action on the 29th, with all eleven available pilots scrambling at 15.50. As the squadron climbed through 10,000 feet they saw some Messerschmitt Me 110s, escorted by Me 109s, which made a single diving attack before turning out to sea to escape to France. Gillam gave chase, and, when just five miles from the French coast, fired all his remaining ammunition into a Me 110, setting both engines on fire before it rolled over and crashed into the sea.

With increasingly fine weather, the Battle now entered into its critical phase, with the tempo of operations increasing daily to a peak that very nearly brought the exhausted Fighter Command pilots to the brink of defeat. But still the remnants of 616 fought on, greatly inspired by the courage and leadership of Denys Gillam, who now showed a fiery and utterly fearless character, which was to make him one of the most distinguished RAF pilots of the war.

Launching at 11.20 on the 30th, eight squadron aircraft were vectored to the Thames Estuary at 17,000 feet, where they saw eighteen Dornier 17s flying in four tight boxes, with the inevitable escort of Me 109s above. All the Spitfires dived at the bombers, some registering hits, but before the results could be observed the Me 109s dropped amongst the squadron and delivered a head-on attack before flying straight through the Spitfire formation. D.S. Smith and Jack Bell turned to meet the enemy, and Smith fired on one of the fighters, which rolled over on its back emitting black smoke before the pilot baled out. Bell was hit in the attack, so he pulled away to head for RAF West Malling for an emergency landing. He crashed on the edge of the airfield and was killed, and so the squadron lost another of its founder members. John Swift Bell, the solicitor from Lincoln, now lies at rest with his mother and father in Lincoln.

Scrambled again at 16.20, nine squadron aircraft climbed over Eastchurch to 23,000 feet to engage a raid of thirty plus bombers with a Me 109 escort. Gillam led Blue Section into an attack on twenty Me 109s, stall-turning onto them. He aimed at the leader and fired a long burst, registering numerous hits. Suddenly the Me 109 stood on its tail and fell out of control to crash near Eastchurch. Gillam hit two more enemy fighters before he in turn came under attack and had to disengage. Throughout the attack, Sergeant J. Hopewell had stuck with Gillam and seen him send one Me 109 down in flames. As another closed in on Blue Leader, Hopewell fired two short bursts, sending the enemy down in flames, the pilot successfully baling out near Eastchurch where he was

Flying Officer Johnnie Bell
(KIA; 29 August 1940).

taken prisoner. In the meantime 'Buck' Casson lost formation after attacking a Me 109, so climbed to 30,000 feet and soon saw about twenty-five Heinkel 111s with an escort of Me 110s heading south on their return to France. He manoeuvred for a front quarter attack on two bombers that were flying together on the outside of the formation, and he dived on them from out of the sun. He fired two long bursts, hitting both, the starboard engine of one almost immediately bursting into flames. Before he could continue his attack he had to dive away as some of the Me 110s turned to counter-attack. On landing from this sortie, the order to scramble 'RADPO' Squadron was to come twice more before the day was over.

The Luftwaffe raids against the south of England became even heavier on the 31st, and Fighter Command losses on this day were the heaviest of the whole Battle. Oddly, 616, although scrambled on two or three occasions, was to see little action on this day of bitter fighting. Four Spitfires took off at 08.45 to patrol Canterbury at 9,000 feet. As they approached their patrol area they saw thirteen Me 109s above them being engaged by another Spitfire squadron, and by the time 616 had gained sufficient height, a hectic dogfight had started. Gillam led his section into the attack, and was able to pick out a Me 109 on the edge of the fight and engage it. He caught the German by surprise and, after his first burst, the enemy aircraft caught fire and the pilot immediately took to his parachute.

As September opened, the Luftwaffe continued its concentrated attacks against the fighter airfields, and on the 1st four major attacks were directed at them with heavy damage being inflicted. 616 was scrambled to meet every attack and, despite being on the front line for just a week, they had suffered such heavy pilot losses that the remaining 'veterans' were flying as many as five sorties a day. Not only did such prodigious flying in the face of the enemy attract immense admiration for the pilots, it was an enormous tribute to the ground crew, the great majority having been recruited locally in South Yorkshire. They too were facing the enemy, as Kenley was subjected to frequent bombing attacks during which they worked tirelessly to prepare aircraft for further flights. The comradeship and trust between the ground crew and 'their' pilots was always a feature of the auxiliary squadrons, and never more so than in 616.

In order to intercept the enemy raids earlier, ten Spitfires took off at 09.00 for the airfield at Hawkinge, on the Kent coast. At 10.30 they were scrambled and told to patrol behind Dover, but en-route they intercepted about thirty Me 109s, which they immediately engaged. In the ensuing dogfight Squadron Leader Robinson gave a Me 109 a short burst and saw it turn on its back, but he did not observe it crash. Flight Sergeant Burnard engaged two enemy fighters, with Casson attacking another. All three pilots were credited with a 'probable', and six more enemy fighters were claimed as damaged. Brewster became detached, so he set off to patrol over Dover where he soon intercepted three Me 109s. He manoeuvred to be able to dive out of the sun, and then he delivered a front quarter attack on the leader and his wingman. He hit the latter, which burst into flames and crashed. Turning to attack the third aircraft from astern, he saw his bullets striking the Me 109 in the fuselage, but before he could complete his attack he was harassed by two further enemy fighters and had to break away. During this raid, Don Smith was hit and injured, and eventually had to abandon his Spitfire.

After returning to Kenley, five Spitfires, led by Gillam, were soon in the air again to patrol over the airfield, as another raid developed. Unable to gain height quickly, Gillam positioned the section to intercept the bombers after their attack, as they were returning to France. The aircraft proved to be Dornier 215 bombers, and Gillam's tactics put his formation in an ideal position to attack from 1,000 feet above. As the Spitfires dived in to attack, the bombers which were flying close together, wheeled towards them, allowing a beam attack to be carried out. Gillam opened fire at 200 yards, and firing continuously, he set one bomber on fire and another dived vertically into the ground. Hopewell singled out another bomber and a short burst sent it crashing to the ground. Attacking from the port quarter, Casson picked out a further Dornier and scored hits on its port wing and fuselage, which ripped open just before the aircraft stalled and dived into the ground. Casson had to break off as a cannon shell exploded in his port wing. He landed his damaged Spitfire safely and two days later, thanks to the sterling work of the tireless ground crew, the aircraft was airborne again. In this short but fierce engagement the five Spitfires had accounted for three bombers and one probable, with a further one damaged. For these pilots it was their fifth combat sortie of the day, a further indication of the intensity and strain of the Battle.

There was to be no let up and, although the squadron saw little action on the 2nd, most of the pilots were scrambled four times during that day, to meet the four main Luftwaffe attacks against the southern airfields. The main activity for 616 occurred late in the afternoon when six Spitfires were ordered to patrol over base. Due to a fault in the station loudspeaker system, two pilots did not hear the order and took off some five minutes after the rest. However, as they climbed to join their colleagues, they intercepted two Me 110s, which were lagging behind a bigger formation. Gillam and his constant No.2, Jim Hopewell, immediately engaged them. Gillam hit one in both engines, and it rolled over in flames, but as he pulled away the second Me 110 hit his Spitfire in the engine. Hopewell promptly turned his attentions to this aircraft and shot it down. As Gillam coaxed his stricken aircraft (X 4181) back to base, at 4,000 feet, the engine suddenly burst into flames and he was forced to bale out. He landed safely in a tree and was soon returned to Kenley.

During the evening of the 2nd, Dowding and his commanders had once again to assess the strength of their depleted squadrons, and Air Vice Marshal Park was forced to rearrange his battle order. The remainder of 616 came to full readiness on the morning of the 3rd, and six aircraft scrambled to patrol over base at 10,000 feet. Shortly afterwards the exhausted remnants were stood down and withdrawn from the front line of the Battle. In the afternoon they flew to RAF Coltishall to be replaced by 66 Squadron. Of the original twenty-one pilots who had flown to Kenley just ten days earlier, only Gillam, Holden, Casson, Murray, Brewster, D.S. Smith, Burnard and Hopewell remained. Four pilots had been killed, five were wounded, one had been made a prisoner of war, one had his commission terminated and another had been posted. Fifteen enemy aircraft had been shot down with a further six claimed as probable, and at least nine had been damaged.

The squadron's departure from Kenley coincided with the end of the 'Third Phase' of the Battle. In the desperate previous two weeks Fighter Command had held back the Luftwaffe's onslaught against the sector airfields and radar sites, but at a terrible cost. Twenty-five per cent of the pilots were lost, and almost 500 fighters were shot down or damaged. Then another colossal blunder by the German High Command gave Dowding

Squadron armourers reload the aircraft's machine-guns.

and his commanders the respite they so desperately needed. The German bombers turned their attention from the fighter airfields and their associated control centres to the capital, London. Fighter Command was saved and, by the end of September, they in turn saved Britain from invasion. Brilliant leadership and control, gallantry of the highest order, and Hitler's great blunder, had ensured that Operation Sealion would never be implemented and, in due course, Germany would lose the war.

CHAPTER FOUR

RECOVERY AND TRAINING

Once 616 had arrived at Coltishall many changes took place. Squadron Leader H.F. 'Billy' Burton, an ex-66 Squadron flight commander and former Cranwell Sword of Honour winner, arrived to take command of the depleted and exhausted squadron. He was to develop an outstanding reputation as a squadron commander and was one of the most popular to lead the squadron. Flight Lieutenants C. Macfie, from 611 (West Lancashire) Squadron, and C.A.T. Jones, from 312 Squadron, arrived to be flight commanders along with a number of young pilots arriving to replace the veterans. They included Pilot Officer J.E. 'Johnnie' Johnson, who was to have a very successful career in 616, achieving even greater fame as the RAF's top-scoring fighter pilot in the Second World War.

On the debit side, the squadron lost its most successful and outstanding Battle of Britain pilot when Flight Lieutenant Denys Gillam was promoted and posted to command 312 (Czech) Squadron. Gillam, the Yorkshireman, was a regular officer, and he had joined 616 to form the small nucleus of regular and experienced pilots shortly after the outbreak of war. A study of the squadron's operations record book reveals his name on almost every page. A natural leader and marksman, he was always at the head of his Flight, leading his young and less experienced pilots into the enemy bomber formations and their fighter escorts. By the end of the Battle he had seven confirmed victories, with a further two probables and at least three damaged. He was to achieve even greater fame leading 615 Squadron on anti-shipping attacks, and later as wing leader of a Typhoon ground attack wing. By the end of the war he was a group captain, having been awarded no less than three DSOs and two DFCs, to add to his pre-war AFC, making him one of the most decorated of all RAF pilots. The squadron also lost Dick Hellyer, who had been with the squadron from the earliest days. He was posted for a 'rest tour' as an instructor on a Spitfire training unit.

After reorganising at RAF Coltishall for a few days, the squadron, equipped with fifteen Spitfires, moved to its permanent home for a few months, at RAF Kirton in Lindsay, Lincolnshire, where it was declared a C Class squadron for a short period. At this time of the Battle, Dowding was forced to classify his fighter squadrons into three types, A, B and C, the latter being used as units to train recently qualified pilots, under the instruction of the remaining veterans, before they were posted south to an A Class squadron. Although still available for emergencies, this was to be the squadron's main role for a number of weeks.

Over the next four months the squadron continued its two roles of training and flying operational patrols. No less than forty-three new pilots joined 616, some straight from the Flying Training Schools, to gain three or four weeks experience before moving south, while others came as experienced pilots from battle-weary squadrons. During early September, the squadron welcomed 'Cocky' Dundas back, recovered from the injuries sustained when he was shot down in August.

During one of the few engagements, the squadron's popular American pilot, Pilot Officer Phil Leckrone, was in company with his flight commander, the boyish-looking twenty-year-old Colin Macfie, when they intercepted a Junkers 88, but their combined fire appeared to do no damage. Sergeant A. Iveson, who was flying as No.3, could not catch his two colleagues. He eventually ran out of fuel and had to ditch alongside a minesweeper. He returned to the squadron via Yarmouth later in the day. Later in the war, Iveson transferred to bombers and was awarded the DFC, serving with 617 Squadron and having flown on the Tirpitz raids.

As the Battle over the southern skies of England continued, the Air Officer Commanding 12 Group, Air Vice Marshal T. Leigh-Mallory, agreed to implement the controversial 'big wing' tactics suggested by Squadron Leader D.R.S. Bader. This involved mustering four or five squadrons over East Anglia, before setting off as a 'balbo' to meet the heavy German air raids; a time-consuming operation. On 19 September, fourteen aircraft from 616 Squadron flew to the satellite airfield of Fowlmere to form part of the Duxford Wing. They flew down each day and, although scrambled on every day to patrol over the Thames Estuary, encountered no action until their second scramble on the 27th. Taking off with 19 Squadron, they climbed to 25,000 feet where they saw fifty plus Me 109s, but as they manoeuvred for position a further twelve Me 109s attacked from the sun. Pilot Officer D.S. Smith, who was weaving behind the squadron, was caught unawares and hit. As the Me 109s attacked, Ken Holden followed one down as it dived past the formation, and gave it a two-second burst at full deflection from 300 yards. The enemy continued to dive and Holden maintained the chase until, within ten miles of the South Coast near Folkstone, he gave the Me 109 a long burst from dead astern, closing to 50 yards. The enemy caught fire, diving into the sea. Sergeant Copeland also engaged a Me 109 and, after a beam attack, the enemy slowed abruptly and its engines almost stopped. Before he could see the outcome, Copeland had to swerve violently to avoid a collision, and so

Flying Officer D.S. Smith
(KIA; 28 September 1940).

he could only claim a probable. He later attacked two more Me 109s and saw his tracers hitting both aircraft before they escaped. Despite serious injuries, Don Smith managed to force-land his Spitfire. He was taken to Faversham Cottage Hospital, but sadly died of his wounds the next day.

On the 29th the squadron was released from its Duxford task and, on the next day, the seven operational pilots of 'B' Flight flew to Ringway for a week to give cover to troop embarkations at Liverpool. They were scrambled on numerous occasions, but saw no activity.

The steady stream of newly trained pilots continued to arrive on the squadron to develop their fighting skills under the tutelage of the veterans. They learned quickly and some of them were to distinguish themselves and win awards, others, sadly, were to be killed in action. The squadron said goodbye to its American friend, Phil Leckrone, who was posted, on 12 October, to Church Fenton to join the first US Eagle Squadron. Sadly he was to be killed in a mid-air collision in the New Year.

More experience was lost to the squadron with the postings of Sergeants Hopewell and Copeland. Both had been stalwarts of the squadron, consistently at the centre of the battle and with many engagements to their credit. A short time later, the squadron was delighted to learn that Hopewell had been awarded the DFM. His citation recorded that 'during day operations he had destroyed at least five enemy aircraft. Sergeant Jim Hopewell has shown courage and determination and has set an excellent example'. Tragically, he was killed in action later in the war. Percy Copeland became an officer and was awarded the DFC, but he was killed in action in the Western Desert, flying a Kittyhawk.

A number of the trainee pilots remained on the squadron to bring it up to full strength, amongst them Pilot Officer P.W.E. 'Nip' Heppell, Sergeants J. McCairns, B. Bingley, D.W. Beedham, R.A. Morton, R.L. Sellars, J.A.H. Jenks, T.F. McDevette and S.W.R. Mabbett.

Training of the new pilots, and numerous abortive scrambles and patrols, were the feature of October and November. Perhaps the number of landing accidents was an indication of the low level of experience of the new pilots. No less than six pilots crashed on landing with most of their aircraft being written off. Fortunately, no one was seriously injured.

Towards the end of October, a lone Heinkel 111 attacked the airfield, dropping six bombs and causing slight damage. A section had been scrambled to intercept but, unfortunately, on this occasion the ground control was poor and the Spitfires failed to find the enemy bomber. However, on 5 November, the squadron was to score its first success for some time when Trevor Jones was scrambled just after 17.00 to intercept a Heinkel 111. As he climbed through 4,500 feet he sighted the bomber just above him heading west, some two miles away. Making good use of the clouds for cover, he climbed to a position 400 yards astern of the enemy before commencing firing, closing to 100 yards and scoring numerous hits. As the bomber started to smoke Jones broke away and, as he did so, bullets smashed into his cockpit, severely wounding him in the right elbow. Despite heavy loss of blood, he landed his aircraft with one hand some thirty minutes later, insisting on making out his report before being taken to Scunthorpe Hospital. Shortly afterwards it was learned that the Heinkel had crashed in the mouth of the Humber. Unfortunately, Jones was unable to return to 616, but he returned to flying duties in due course, and was awarded a DFC for later exploits. Ken Holden was promoted to command 'A' Flight.

The next day saw the return of Roy Marples, another of the squadron's injured Battle of Britain pilots.

On 8 November the squadron was scrambled twice. Whilst climbing on the second one, the recently arrived young Pilot Officer Ralph Roberts lost control of his aircraft at 19,000 feet. The speed of his uncontrolled dive was such that the wings were torn from his Spitfire (X 4056) before it struck the ground. He was killed. The cause was never determined, but it was thought that he may have suffered from lack of oxygen and fainted.

On the same day the squadron welcomed two Polish pilots, Flight Lieutenant Pietraszkiowicz, and Pilot Officer Lukavzewicz, who had recently been flying Defiants.

Training new pilots and operating patrols continued as the routine of November and December. Late in November news came that the recently posted Denys Gillam had been awarded the DFC for outstanding leadership, aggressive spirit and courage throughout the Battle of Britain, whilst commanding 'A' Flight of the squadron. There could hardly have been a more deserving or popular award.

Towards the end of November, the squadron commander, Billy Burton, wrote to the *Chester Herald* at the College of Arms, to resurrect the issue of a squadron badge.

Pilots at Kirton-in-Lindsay, November 1940. *Standing, left to right:* unknown, Morton (POW), Bingley (KIA), unknown, Holden, Hepple, Burton (CO), Macfie (POW), Mabbett (KIA), Le Cheminant, unknown, Pietraszkiowicz. *Front:* Sellars (KIA), McDevette (KIA), Brewster, Casson (POW) McCairns (POW, Escaped), Roberts (KIA), Jenks (KIA).

The first CO, Squadron Leader the Earl of Lincoln, had first approached the *Chester Herald* regarding the design of a squadron badge a few weeks after the formation of the squadron. In seeking advice, he also enquired about the suitability of depicting the 'head of a war horse clad in armour' in green and gold. The *Chester Herald* thought this appropriate, adding a further suggestion that the badge depict the lower half of the white rose of Yorkshire, signifying South Yorkshire, with an arrow pointing due north, and the motto 'TAQUAM SAGITTA', which translates to 'like an arrow'.

The idea of using the Yorkshire rose appealed to the Earl of Lincoln, but he preferred using a full rose with the arrow in bend (pointing to the north-west). When queried on this latter detail, the Earl claimed it indicated speed and attack. The *Chester Herald* was less sure on this point, preferring an arrow pointing north. After more correspondence, the Earl of Lincoln's view prevailed, together with the alternative motto, 'NULLA ROSA SINE SPINA', translated as 'no rose without a thorn'. Shortly afterwards, the Second World War broke out and the squadron commander suggested the design of the badge should be decided once the war was over and the matter was closed.

When Billy Burton wrote to the *Chester Herald* on 20 November, he submitted two further designs. These had been designed and drawn by L.A.C. Debenham, an airmen of 616, and depicted the white rose of Yorkshire and a three-bladed propeller. However, once the *Chester Herald* outlined its previous proposals, the squadron commander immediately agreed to the original design and motto. In early February 1941, the Chief of the Air Staff approved the design. The original was submitted with the words 'South Yorkshire (F) Squadron', but this was eschewed on security grounds. His Majesty the King approved the design in June 1941.

Following the great German night Blitz on Sheffield, the squadron spent much of December patrolling over its 'own city'. Numerous scrambles were ordered, but no contact was made with the enemy. These patrols culminated in a goodwill flypast over the city on Christmas Eve, and the formation carried on flying over Doncaster, Worksop and Welbeck. So ended a momentous year for the squadron in which they had graduated from being a non-operational squadron to a battle-hardened one.

The beginning of 1941 saw the first engagements by the squadron for some time. Colin Macfie caught a Heinkel 111 forty miles out to sea, and got in two long bursts before the enemy disappeared into cloud. A few days later, John Brewster had a similar experience with a Dornier 17. On 15 January, Red Section was scrambled to 2,000 feet to protect a convoy from hostile aircraft approaching from the east. 'Cocky' Dundas and his No.2, 'Johnnie' Johnson, attacked a Dornier, silencing the rear gunner and damaging it. Poor weather prevented flying, but the popular Roy Marples celebrated his twenty-first birthday by inviting all the officers to a celebration dinner in the officers' mess. The squadron diarist noted that 'there was no doubt that everybody thoroughly enjoyed themselves'! Sadly, the squadron said goodbye to its two Polish officers, 'Piet' going to command a Hurricane squadron at RAF Acklington.

Frustration became the feature of February, with poor weather and numerous inconclusive scrambles and interceptions. The squadron log records that the 'pilots are becoming restive'. By the end of the month, the squadron had said goodbye to one of its stalwart original auxiliaries when Pilot Officer John Brewster was posted to 118 Squadron, a recently formed squadron at Filton. Then came the exciting news that 616

'Nip' Hepple, Roy Marples and 'Johnnie' Johnson at Kirton-in-Lindsay, January 1941.

was to move back to the frontline. After a farewell dinner with the popular station commander of Kirton in Lindsay, Wing Commander S.H. Hardy, fourteen squadron aircraft took off for RAF Tangmere, near Chichester in Sussex, on 26 February. The squadron took over from 65 Squadron, and inherited their new Spitfire IIAs. Thus started one of the most hectic periods in the history of the squadron.

CHAPTER FIVE

TANGMERE WING

The squadron arrived at Tangmere as Fighter Command had started to go on the offensive over northern France. Small groups of fighters crossed the English Channel to shoot up airfields, roads and rail transport targets. These tactics were developed during the New Year with the aim of attracting the Luftwaffe into the air, but to entice the German fighters some form of bait was needed. Light bombers, initially Blenheims of 2 Group, were escorted to a target with the sole intention of being bait. Hence, the 'circus' operation was born, where a small bomber force was given a heavy fighter escort in the hope that the Luftwaffe would attack the bombers, allowing the escort fighters to engage them in combat. On these RAF operations, up to thirty-six fighters would rendezvous with the bombers, flying at 12,000 feet, the maximum height for flak at that time. They were enveloped by these close support fighters to form the 'beehive'. Other fighters, the support wings, flew above the beehive, and were free to engage any German fighters. 616 would fly many of these operations in the weeks ahead.

Variations on this type of operation were developed and became known as 'sweeps', the type of sweep being given a name depending on the size and type of force used. A 'rodeo' was a sweep over enemy territory without bombers. A 'ramrod' was a similar operation to a circus, but where the objective was the destruction of a specific target. Finally, a 'rhubarb' was a small-scale freelance operation, usually flown in poor weather, with the aim of attacking targets of opportunity. These operations were just becoming established when 616 Squadron appeared on the stage.

Also resident at the pre-war airfield outside Chichester were 145 and 610 Squadrons, and the three units together formed the Tangmere Wing. The first two weeks were taken up with training exercises, battle formation climbs and practise wing operations. In addition, the squadron was tasked to maintain two aircraft at readiness, and run a number of patrols over the South Coast and the Isle of Wight. On 10 March 616 flew its first sweep, operating in the Calais – Boulogne area at 31,000 feet, but saw no action. On the return, Sergeant B. Bingley crashed near Worthing and was killed, thus becoming the squadron's first casualty of 1941.

The arrival, on 18 March, of Wing Commander D.R.S. Bader DSO, DFC, at Tangmere, marked an important day in the history of 616 Squadron. Throughout his time as the Tangmere Wing leader, he would lead flying with 616 and his personal Spitfire, which carried the code D-B, rather than the squadron code at the time, QJ, was serviced by 'A' Flight. He lost no time in making his dynamic presence felt when the following day he led the Wing for the first time. During a sweep at 30,000 feet, south of Beachy Head, two Me 109s made a quick attack. Johnnie Johnson called 'Look out!' and the formation scattered. After a public rebuke on landing, and a wry smile from Bader, the lesson was hammered home, and Johnson went on to have a glittering career.

In addition to the offensive sweeps, the squadron was also heavily committed to flying defensive patrols over the South Coast. The squadron's first success came on 27 March, when twenty-year-old Colin Macfie was scrambled with Sergeant R.L. Sellars to patrol base at 15,000 feet. The two Spitfires were vectored to a 'bogey' approaching the area of Arundel. Macfie attacked a Messerschmitt Me 110, hitting one of the enemy fighter's engines. Oil splattered over the cockpit of Macfie's Spitfire so he was unable to press home the attack. This meant he could only claim a 'damaged'. Sellars had to make a forced landing near Durrington, owing to a faulty petrol gauge, radio failure and the misting up of his cockpit.

On 1 April, the squadron welcomed two New Zealand pilots, when Sergeants R.L. Brewer and J.C. West arrived from an Operational Training Unit.

'Buck' Casson and Ken Holden at Tangmere in April 1941.

Tangmere suffered a heavy air raid on 8 April, and one of the airman's blocks received a direct hit, killing six personnel, with others being injured. The station also came under machine-gun attack from low-flying aircraft and the ground crew soon realised that they too were in the combat area, and at risk.

Bader drove his squadrons hard, using his own aggressive spirit to generate morale. The Wing developed a great spirit of camaraderie, an essential ingredient for success. Typifying the mood was the recently arrived Sergeant Bob 'Butch' Morton, who hailed from Hull. He used a part of the city's coat of arms to adorn his Mae West life jacket, and the fin of his Spitfire held the motto, 'Spotto, Squirto, Scrammo' which translated to 'I spot, I fire, I remove myself'! Bader approved. The squadron's 'A' Flight adorned their hut with the notice 'Bader's Bus Company. Daily trips to the Continent. Return Tickets Only'. The Wing soon adopted the motto 'Bader's Bus Company'.

On 21 April the Wing escorted eighteen Blenheims to Le Havre. The operation did not go well, and the Spitfires had to return short of fuel. Over the Channel, a Me 109 hit Sergeant Sellars' Spitfire, and he was forced to bale out. Macfie and Morton circled him as he floated in the water and transmitted for a fix. The squadron refuelled and eight Spitfires immediately left to search the area and escort a Lysander air-sea rescue aircraft, but no trace was found of Sellars, the squadron's first casualty to enemy fire since the Battle of Britain.

Three days later, Macfie and Sergeant T.F. McDevette took off to strafe aircraft on Maupertas airfield, near Cherbourg. They machine-gunned seven Me 109s on the ground, and attacked two others as they took off. On their return journey, somewhere near the coast, McDevette, who had been with 616 for six months, disappeared and failed to return. His body was never recovered. He is remembered on the Runnymede Memorial.

Training, convoy patrols and defensive sweeps became the routine operations for the squadron. On 5 May, Roy Marples and 'Buck' Casson were scrambled to intercept a contact approaching the Portsmouth area. Flying at 15,000 feet they intercepted a Ju 88, closing in just as the enemy bomber dived to sea level and turned for France. Marples was slightly ahead and opened fire first, and then Casson's fire silenced the enemy gunner, but two further attacks appeared to have no effect as the Junkers pilot evaded them. As happened so often in combat, Casson suddenly found himself alone, so he climbed to 7,000 feet and headed for Tangmere. As he descended he noticed that the engine oil temperature was rising, and it was losing its glycol coolant. He had just crossed the coast when the engine stopped and the cockpit filled with smoke, so he inverted the aircraft at 950 feet and baled out, landing behind some council houses near Littlehampton. The British community in Buenos Aires had donated his aircraft (P 7753), to be called *Pampero One*.

A few days later, on 9 May, the squadron moved a few miles to the grass satellite airfield at Westhampnett to join 610 Squadron. The small airfield near Goodwood was to remain the home of 616 until it moved north later in the year. Facilities were spartan, with the squadron headquarters in a marquee behind the 'A' Flight dispersal area, and rustic wooden huts served as the briefing and crew rooms. Within two days, Tangmere, where the ground crew remained billeted, came under more machine-gun attacks, and sleeping quarters for some of the squadron personnel moved to Goodwood House on top of the Sussex Downs.

For some time, the squadron pilots had been concerned about the rigid formation tactics employed by Fighter Command, and much discussion took place on how a more

NCO pilots at Woodfield House, Tangmere, May 1941. *Left to right:* Mabbett, A. Smith, Brewer (NZ), West (NZ).

flexible approach could be adopted. A significant engagement during a morning sortie on the 8th merely reinforced their view. The previous evening 'Cocky' Dundas had suggested that four aircraft should fly line abreast and, in this way, be able to cover the tails of each other. Bader decided to try the idea, and he led four aircraft on a sweep south of Dover, at 26,000 feet. Six Me 109s closed in on the Spitfires. Bader held his order to break until the last minute, when the four fighters pulled into a steep turn. Dundas was hit and smoke poured from his aircraft. However, one of the pilots (from 610 Squadron) shot a Me 109 down, and Dundas was able to limp into Hawkinge where he completed a high-speed belly landing, which badly damaged his Spitfire (P 7827), the *Cock of the North*.

When Dundas returned to Manston, the four pilots discussed the engagement and realised that the call to break had come too late, but that the principle was correct. The original formation was modified slightly to two pairs of aircraft line abreast but slightly staggered, and hence the 'finger four' formation was born, which soon became standard practice for the majority of fighter squadrons.

Each day saw plenty of flying activity for the squadron, with convoy patrols over the Solent and standing patrols over base and over the English Channel, all being regular operations. Scrambles to intercept possible targets were a daily occurrence. Training was always a high priority and the new tactic of flying in finger four required developing and refining, with battle climbs in sections of four being particularly important. Dog fighting and cine-gun practise featured almost every day.

On 17 May, Dundas and Sergeant R.L. Brewer were returning from a patrol over the Channel when they were ordered to investigate three contacts. Dundas' combat report gives the details of the engagement:

> Sent to investigate three bogeys south of Shoreham at 14,000 feet. Climbed line abreast with Red 2 and passing 7,000 feet saw three Me 109s. Climbed to attack when one aircraft detached and attacked Red 2 giving him a long burst from astern and close. As it broke away, I fired a two- to three-second burst with full deflection and extreme range but had to break off as other 2 e/a closed in. Later confirmed a Me 109 crashed in the sea.

Unseasonable weather interfered with operations for the latter part of May, and it was not until 3 June that the squadron flew another offensive sweep over the Dunkirk – Boulogne area, but no enemy were contacted.

On 4 June, the squadron said goodbye to one of its longest-serving members, when Ken Holden was promoted to squadron leader and moved across the airfield to command 610 Squadron. He was replaced by Flight Lieutenant E.P.P. Gibbs, a flying instructor with no combat experience, but an ace aerobatic pilot. Even Bader, who considered himself to be an expert at aerobatics, was envious of his skills, in particular Gibbs' brilliant execution of the difficult third upward roll, which he seemed able to perform with ease. It did not endear him to Bader!

During the middle of the month, two squadron airmen distinguished themselves in a very brave action. After the Spitfires had returned from a sortie, the armourers started to empty the ammunition tanks. An explosion occurred in one of the tanks, and Keighley-born Aircraftman Kenneth Bland climbed onto the wing of the Spitfire, despite the explosions, and unfastened the gun panels. The ammunition tank was burning furiously, so he released the gun. Sergeant George Williams rushed to the scene and removed the burning tank, which continued to explode as he carried it away. Both these gallant airmen were awarded the George Medal. The citation concluded, 'The presence of mind and courage shown by these two airmen undoubtedly saved the aircraft and probably the lives of the air crews and armourers who were attempting to release the remaining ammunition tanks.' The 616 Squadron airmen on the ground matched the bravery of their pilots in the air.

In June the weather was superb, and the Tangmere Wing was busy on bomber escort duties, flying patrols and sweeps, but the Luftwaffe fighters were reluctant to engage. A crop of new pilots arrived, amongst them a number from the Commonwealth. Early June also marked a significant shift of emphasis for the squadrons of Fighter Command, based in the south of England. This can best be explained by the entry in the squadron operations record book for 10 June:

> A period of glorious weather and intense activity over Northern France commences. In all the Tangmere Wing patrols, W.Cdr Bader flies with us and leads the Wing. We are the bottom squadron, 610 Squadron next and No.145 on top. All these wing patrols are to cover bombers over Northern France.

A few days earlier, Germany had started to mass its divisions on the Polish – Russian border, and on 21 June Hitler launched Operation Barbarossa against Russia. It was not known how many Luftwaffe units had been transferred to the Eastern Front, but there was a clear Air Ministry directive to maintain the pressure on German forces based in northern France. The Commander-in-Chief of Fighter Command, Air Marshal Sir Sholto Douglas, believed this could best be achieved by continuing the offensive over France, in order to force the Luftwaffe to leave fighter units in the west. Circus operations, with strong fighter support, continued to be mounted in an attempt to force the Luftwaffe to retain fighters in the west, thus relieving the struggling Russians.

After a relatively quiet period during the early days of June operations intensified considerably, and 21 June marked the beginning of a very hectic two months. The squadron saw a great deal more action, with four patrols and two full wing patrols being flown over northern France. The squadron commander, Squadron Leader Billy Burton, shared in the destruction of a Me 109. Just after taking off, the hood of his Spitfire came adrift, and he had to land again to have it fixed. Ten minutes later he was airborne, and climbed to 20,000 feet over Dungeness, where he saw two Me 109s being attacked by a Spitfire. He joined in and a dogfight developed. Both Spitfires had made a number of attacks when the enemy pilot jettisoned his canopy and baled out. The pilot, Oberfeldwebel Luders of *6/JG26*, became a POW.

'A' Flight at Westhampnett, June 1941. *Standing, left to right:* Johnson, Mabbett, Scott, McCairns. *Seated:* Dundas, Hepple, A.Smith.

Later in the day, Bader led the Wing on a bomber escort operation. As the bombers left the target near Boulogne, Bader's section was attacked by two Me 109s. Breaking left and turning rapidly, Bader fired a very close deflection shot from 50 yards. Bullets hit the canopy of the enemy fighter and it pulled up vertically, stalled and went into a spin. The pilot baled out and the aircraft crashed into the sea. It was Bader's first success on a sweep.

During this operation the squadron suffered its first officer casualty since moving south, when Pilot Officer E.P.S. Brown was seen diving out of control north-west of Boulogne. He failed to return. The following day, Sergeant D.W. Beedham ran out of fuel returning from a sweep, and he was forced to bale out near Brighton. The air-sea rescue organisation picked him up from the Channel and he was quickly returned to the squadron.

The following day brought more success for 616. An offensive wing patrol was launched during the afternoon, when a force of Me 109s was intercepted over northern France. Roy Marples was flying as Blue 3 on the starboard side of the squadron. The combat report takes up the story:

> In a shallow dive, sighted 3 Me 109s in line astern positioning to attack Blue Section. Called leader but got no answer so broke away. Me 109s saw him coming so commenced hard port turn. Closed on No.3 to 200 yards and gave 2 to 3 bursts from port quarter. Wobbled as other 2 dived away. Two more bursts and the enemy went into a spin. Followed him down, spinning all the way, then had to break off as 2 Me 109s returned.

Marples was credited with a kill. During the same action, 'Buck' Casson, leading Sergeant Beedham, picked out a lone Me 109 and attacked it. After two deflection shots, Casson tightened the turn and got in two more bursts as the Me 109's engine started to windmill as the fighter lost speed. It turned over on its back, apparently out of control, and crashed.

The 25th proved to be an eventful day for the squadron. Bader led the Wing at noon to provide cover for a circus operation. Just after crossing the French coast, a large force of Me 109s engaged the Spitfires. During a major fight, Bader claimed to have destroyed an enemy fighter and shared a second with the New Zealander, Sergeant Jeff West. Flight Lieutenant Gibbs and Sergeant Brewer claimed a probable each, and Dundas and Marples claimed a damaged.

Just before 16.00 the Wing took off to escort Circus 23, a force of Blenheims attacking St Omer. Just after crossing the French coast, twelve Me 109s were engaged, and pilots of 145 and 610 Squadrons had some success, but it was a bad day for 616. Bader and his No.2 attacked a group of four fighters near Boulogne. He gave one a short burst at close range, and it went down vertically, streaming smoke. After a great struggle to release himself, the pilot, Oberleutnant Heinz Gottlob of *I/JG 26*, was able to bale out, but was badly wounded and never returned to flying operations. Roy Marples and Sergeant Bob Morton were attacked, and Morton's aircraft was hit. He described what happened:

> We were jumped from behind. There was the usual display of golden rain accompanied by sundry bangs as cannon shells exploded inside the machine. Instinctively I rolled on to my back and went vertically down as the cockpit filled with smoke. I pulled out of the dive as

'Buck' Casson with his ground crew, Lee Marshall and Jack Atkinson at Westhampnett, June 1941.

the smoke eased but the engine sounded like a cement mixer. I quickly throttled back and surveyed the instruments. The radiator temperature was jammed against the upper stop, as was the oil temperature. The oil pressure needle had dropped below the scale. My only hope was to hold a northerly course towards the Channel where I would have a chance of being picked up by our Air-Sea Rescue. However, against all reason the magnificent Rolls-Royce Merlin kept going and I crossed the Channel and managed to land at Hawkinge in a series of ungainly hops.

The miraculous escape of Bob Morton was tempered by the loss of Sergeant J. Jenks and the New Zealander Sergeant R.L. Brewer. Twenty-five-year-old Jenks, who had been with the squadron since March, had been shot down over St Omer and was buried at Boulogne. It was believed that Brewer had become detached from the formation south of Le Touquet, and was shot down. He was lost without trace, and is commemorated on the Runnymede Memorial.

The following day 616 mounted one sweep which was notable because it provided the first of 'Johnnie' Johnson's many successes, which would make him the highest-scoring

RAF pilot by the end of the war. His combat report, written in a matter-of-fact way, explains the action:

> I became detached from Wing Commander Bader's section at 15,000 feet through watching three 109s immediately above me. I saw them dive away to port and almost immediately afterwards saw an Me 109E coming in from my starboard side and which flew across me about 150 yards away, turning slightly to port. I immediately turned inside the enemy aircraft (E/A) and opened fire, closing to 100 yards. After two one-second bursts the E/A jettisoned its hood, rolled over and the pilot baled out, his parachute opening almost immediately. I then broke away as there were other E/A about. I estimated I was over Gravelines when in combat. On landing I heard that several pilots of 145 Squadron had witnessed this. After the combat I joined up with Flying Officer Scott of 145 Squadron and we landed at Hawkinge to refuel, returning to Westhampnett at 13.25 Hours.

'Buck' Casson managed to damage another Me 109, but Bob Morton had yet more adventures. He became very disorientated on his return from the same sweep, and mistook the northern shore of the Thames Estuary for the south coast of the Isle of White. He headed north and, before finding an airfield, ran out of fuel in Norfolk and was forced to land in a field where his Spitfire (P 7815) was wrecked.

Escorting circus operations continued over the next few days, but 616 saw little action. On 30 June, Sergeant 'Mac' McCairns had a lucky escape when a bullet exploded in the cockpit of his Spitfire. He was uninjured, and was able to return safely. 'Buck' Casson was promoted to flight lieutenant and took command of 'A' Flight. During this period Lieutenant Montgomery of the USAAF was attached to the squadron for a week, and he flew on a number of air-to-air firing practises, but before gaining any operational experience was suddenly recalled.

The arrival of July heralded the most hectic few months in the history of 616. Sweeps over northern France continued on an almost daily basis. Following the interrogation of a captured German fighter pilot, Fighter Command were made aware that Luftwaffe pilots had instructions not to attack Spitfires if they were acting alone, since they would not be carrying bombs. However, if the RAF aircraft were escorting bombers, the Luftwaffe pilots had orders to engage. This information confirmed the value of using bombers as bait to entice the German fighters into the air, allowing the escorting Spitfire squadrons to engage.

On 2 July the Wing escorted bombers to Lille and became involved in a major dogfight with Me 109s of *JG26*. Bader was leading 616 when he sighted fifteen enemy fighters and turned the squadron to attack. He attacked an Me 109F and saw the pilot jettison the hood and prepare to bale out, but he had to break away at that point as another Me 109 was closing in. He fired on it and saw glycol stream from its engine, but he did not see it go down. On landing, Bader claimed one fighter as destroyed and the other as damaged. Pilot Officer Philip 'Nip' Heppell, flying in Bader's section, also shot down a fighter. Sergeant Alan Smith, Bader's No.2, also claimed one destroyed and one damaged.

During the day it was announced that Bader had been awarded a Bar to his DSO. The squadron was delighted to learn that Ken Holden, one of the squadron's first auxiliaries, and now commanding 610 Squadron with the Tangmere Wing, had been awarded the DFC.

The following day, Sergeant Douglas Crabtree, who had only been with the squadron since mid-May, failed to return from a circus operation to Hazebrouck. He was forced to bale out of his burning Spitfire (P 7980), and after many weeks on the run, returned to England via Spain, visiting the squadron in September to relate his experiences. The Canadian Sergeant R.D. 'Trapper' Bowen had a narrow escape when he attacked a Henschel Hs 126 observation aircraft. Misjudging the slow speed of the aircraft, his wing tip clipped the wing strut of the Hs 126, and it spiralled away. Bowen returned safely and claimed a probable.

Bader achieved another success on 5 July when he engaged an Me 109E south of Gravelines. He closed to 20 yards, whilst firing, and almost collided with the enemy fighter, which appeared to have been hit as it fell away, seemingly out of control. The CO, Billy Burton, saw the engagement and confirmed that the Me 109 had crashed. Its pilot, Leutnant Joachim Kerhahn of *I/JG26*, did not survive. The squadron suffered a severe loss when Colin Macfie, the flight commander of 'A' Flight, was shot down. He was seen to bale out of his Spitfire (P 8651), which carried the name *St Helens*, having been gifted by the people of the Lancashire town. Some time later he was reported as a prisoner of war. He had been with the squadron since the previous September and had been a very effective pilot and flight commander. The squadron diarist spoke for everyone on the squadron when he recorded:

> An offensive wing patrol at lunchtime from which F/Lt Macfie did not return. We were all very sad at his loss for he had been with the squadron since the beginning of September 1940, and he had endeared himself to everyone despite his taciturnity. We heard later that he sprained his ankle when landing by parachute, and is in a Prisoner of War Camp.

A few weeks later it was announced that he had been awarded the DFC. Casson took over 'B' Flight and 'Cocky' Dundas was promoted to take over 'A' Flight.

The pattern of activities over the next few days was virtually the same. Bader led the Wing on offensive sweeps, sometimes two per day, usually escorting the new four-engine bomber, the Short Stirling. The squadron was in combat on all these sorties, and some successes were achieved. Bader and 'Johnnie' Johnson each made a claim on 6 July, but one of the squadron's long-serving and most effective sergeant pilots, 'Mac' McCairns failed to return. He was seen to crash-land his Spitfire (P 8500) on the beach at Dunkirk. He was slightly injured and taken prisoner, but it was far from the end of his war. In January 1942 he escaped from Stalag IXC, south of Berlin, and during an epic three-month journey managed to get to Spain, with the help of the gallant members of the Belgian 'Comet' Line. He was awarded the Military Medal, and returned to operations as a Lysander pilot with the 'Moonlight Squadron', delivering and picking up agents from fields in France. He was awarded the DFC three times.

The stress of combat also affected the ground crew. The fitters and riggers became very attached to 'their' aircraft, and their pilots and all the members of the squadron shared their concerns. Dennis Hill captured the feelings of all the ground crew:

'Cocky' Dundas. and his ground crew Harry Mason and Ken Goodlad.

It was always an anxious time when the planes took off as we knew they had to be back in two hours time [the maximum time for Spitfires to remain in the air]. At times during these flights we would look skyward to the south to see if we could spot the aircraft returning and see if the cloth covering over the guns had been torn, which indicated the guns had been fired. When the planes came back in ones and twos, we just waited to see if all 12 were back at base.

On 8 July, the squadron started to re-equip with the Spitfire VB, a significant improvement on the Mark IIA, with four of the latter's eight machine-guns being replaced with two of the much more effective 40mm Hispano-Suiza cannon. New pilots, many of them young sergeants, kept arriving, and their training in tactics generated much of the flying. There was a hard core of experienced pilots: Burton, Casson, Dundas, Heppell, Johnson, Marples, Smith and West. They were the regulars on the offensive sweeps, with the less experienced tending to fly the convoy and base patrols.

Bader and his wingman, Alan Smith, each destroyed an Me 109 on 9 July, but Pat Gibbs and Bob Morton both failed to return. Morton, for the second time, experienced 'golden rain' in his cockpit, after being attacked from behind. Unfortunately, this time his engine

Douglas Bader at Westhampnett a week before he was shot down. *Left to right:* Johnson, Dundas, Bader, Lt Montgomery (USAAF).

seized and he was forced to make a wheels-up landing in a large field near St Omer. He spent the rest of the war as a prisoner.

The aerobatic ace, Pat Gibbs, had an altogether different experience. After his aircraft was crippled, he started to glide towards a field for a belly landing, but, noticing that German fighters were closing in on him, inverted his Spitfire (P 8070) to give the impression he was crashing out of control. At the last minute he rolled the aircraft and made a perfect landing in a field south of Le Touquet. He got away before the Germans arrived, and made his way south, eventually reaching Spain. He arrived back in England in September, three months after being shot down. He returned to operations in command of 130 Squadron, and was awarded the DFC in January 1941.

10 July was a busy day. The squadron provided seven aircraft for a high cover patrol, circus operation, to Bethune. Bader's Dogsbody section encountered several Me 109s, which they attacked. Bader claimed a probable. As they left the Calais region they spotted three more of the fighters and closed in for the attack. 'Nip' Heppel, who was flying as the No.4, recorded:

I was Dogsbody 4 flying in W/Cdr Bader's section and being number two to F/Lt Dundas. The Wing was patrolling in the Calais area just prior to returning to Tangmere, when we sighted a section of 3 Me 109s several thousand feet below travelling in the opposite direction in a wide vic. We did a half roll and dived after them attaining a speed of about 400. We were diving almost line abreast. Wing Commander Bader on the left, Flight Lieutenant Dundas in the centre and myself on the right. I was slightly further back than the other two. The e/a on the right, which I was attacking, saw the other two [Spitfires] delivering their attack and turned to the left just as I was about to fire. I fired at him on the turn for a few seconds (at 200 yards) and then broke under him. By this time he was going down in a gentle dive with glycol streaming from him.

The steady arrival, throughout July, of the Spitfire VB, caused some problems, testing the patience of the ground crew. The diarist of the squadron's operational record book captured the situation and highlighted the sterling work provided by the ground crew:

Unfortunately the Armament and Maintenance sections experienced considerable difficulty with the cannons and engines, due to poor workmanship and faulty installation. The people responsible for seeing that the new aircraft sent out to operational units are fit to fly and fight in little realise the difficulties that the maintenance staffs have to contend with. In some cases it took a week before the aircraft was finally passed out for operational use. All this extra work had to be done during a period of intense activity, and no praise is too high for all the men engaged in a task which is usually taken for granted and receives very little recognition.

The pilots would echo those final sentiments. In conversations with the author, 'Buck' Casson, 'Cocky' Dundas and Johnnie Johnson were full of praise for their ground crew. Each of them established a particularly close and loyal bond with their fitter and rigger, remaining close friends with them for the duration of their lives.

During a sweep over northern France, on 11 July, Alan Smith found another way to attack the enemy. His oxygen system was faulty and he had to leave the formation and descend to a lower altitude. He saw an airfield near St Omer packed with Junker Ju 87 Stuka dive-bombers. He dived to attack, and gave a long burst from his cannons as he flew along the length of the parked aircraft, hitting some and seeing flames emitted from two of them. He had alerted the airfield defences during his first surprise attack, so he decided it would not be prudent to go for a second pass. As he departed he was heartened to see a French woman waving to him as he sped for the coast and back across the Channel.

Bader added another Me 109 to his ever-growing list of successes on the next day. During a morning offensive sweep at 26,000 feet, his formation encountered twelve to fifteen enemy fighters near St Omer. In a short and fierce engagement he damaged two, before attacking a pair that were threatening the beehive. He damaged one and saw the second burst into flames. He claimed one destroyed and three damaged. Smith also claimed a probable.

'Johnnie' Johnson gained his third success on 14 July, when he destroyed an Me 109F during a bomber escort operation to Hazebrouck. His combat report gives the details:

I became separated from the squadron when over the target, so decided to fly with the Beehive during the return flight. When about 25-30 miles from the French coast and flying at 1,500 feet above and behind the Beehive, I saw three aircraft in line astern to the south-west. I then turned inland, above and behind the three aircraft, which I then identified as Me1 09Fs. I made a quick aileron turn and attacked No.3 from below and behind, when I was climbing. I gave a second burst with cannon and machine-gun at 150 yards range and saw the tail unit blown off and the E/A went into an uncontrollable spin. I am claiming this E/A as destroyed. I then broke away as my No.2 had lost me.

19 July saw Bader leading the Wing on a target support operation. There was a brief encounter with Me 109s over Dunkirk, and Bader claimed one destroyed while sharing in the destruction of a second, with 'Cocky' Dundas. Casson claimed a probable. Later in the day there was much rejoicing when news was received that Dundas, one of the squadron's originals, was awarded the DFC. He was the first of the original members of 616 to receive this honour while serving with the squadron. The citation said: 'This officer has shown unflagging courage in the face of the enemy and the utmost tenacity in supporting his leader.'

Alan Smith with Flight Lieutenant Gibbs, the squadron's intelligence officer.

The life of a fighter squadron in the front line was always one of contrasts. Two days after the celebration of Dundas's DFC, the reality of air fighting, and flying high-performance fighters, was once again highlighted. During a circus operation to Lens that evening most of the pilots were in action during a series of fierce fights, and a number claimed probables and damaged. 'Johnnie' Johnson's regular No.2, Sergeant S. W. R. 'George' Mabbett, was shot down and killed in P 8690. A fine rugby player, the twenty-two-year-old pilot was buried at Longuenesse Souvenir Cemetery, where the Germans accorded him a full military funeral with honours. Johnson had established a close rapport with Mabbett, and he was deeply moved by his loss. Later that day, during a routine training flight, Sergeant F.A. Nelson, who was a new arrival, was killed near Worthing when his Spitfire (P 8434) failed to recover from a spin.

Twelve new Spitfire VBs arrived in the squadron on the 22nd. During the following evening there was an intensive engagement with Me 109s. 'Johnnie' Johnson recorded in his log book: 'More 109s about than ever before. Wing engagements almost whole time over France.' Just after crossing the coast near Le Touquet, German fighters attacked the Wing, which split into smaller groups. Some estimates claimed that over fifty enemy fighters were involved. Bader shared in the destruction of an Me 109 with a pilot from 610 Squadron, and, a short time later, the wing leader shared another with 'Cocky' Dundas. 'Buck' Casson destroyed one and damaged two, and Johnson damaged a third. Casson's combat report prepared with the squadron's long-serving intelligence officer, Flight Lieutenant C.R. Gibbs, gives a graphic description of his engagement:

I was Blue 1, leading a section of four aircraft to port of and above the squadron. As we approached the French coast over Le Touquet at 22,000 feet the leading section broke up after somebody had informed the leader that he was about to be attacked from the rear ... we were ordered to continue our course inland with the result that my section was flying a mile ahead of the wing.

Several enemy aircraft passed over us when we were about fifteen miles inland, but did not attack, and, upon reaching Hazebrouck Wood, about thirty Me 109Fs were seen climbing up directly behind us in a very ragged formation. We split in to two pairs and I turned to port with my No.2 (P/O Trench) and dived on the last two E/As which were in line astern and lagging slightly, giving two bursts of approximately two seconds each, one from about 350 yards and the other from 200 yards as the deflection decreased. The last aircraft turned over and dived away emitting black smoke and I lost sight of it in the haze as it dived down directly over Hazebrouck Wood. My No.2 who engaged these aircraft with me saw pieces fall from it as it dived away.

Breaking right I climbed again and looked out for my No.2 but couldn't see him. He saw me however and was climbing up to rejoin when four Me 109s crossed his path and he followed them. After weaving about for a short time, I decided to make for the coast again and saw two Me 109s climbing up about 2,000 feet below me. I went into a half roll and tried to engage them but was travelling too fast and couldn't get my sights to bear on either of them. They didn't see my first effort and it was not until I had crossed behind them and was diving again from the port quarter that they saw me. They broke upwards in opposite directions and I opened up at the nearer aircraft from 300 yards and closing to about 100 yards, with one long burst. White smoke suddenly poured from his engine and turning very steeply he dived almost vertically leaving a trail of white and black smoke. I followed him down to about 7,000 feet and saw him crash close to a small wood on the south side of Abbeville and burst into flames. I then turned north for home and hit the coast at Dungeness.

Casson's claim was a cause for celebration as it was registered as the squadron's fiftieth success.

A period of bad weather set in, and few patrols were possible. Johnnie Johnson thought this respite was much needed. He was concerned that Bader, in particular, who insisted on leading every sweep and had completed more than any other pilot, was reaching exhaustion, and it was obvious that others too were showing the strain. Some had been on almost continuous operations since the Battle of Britain, including Casson, Dundas, Marples and Johnson himself. During this quieter period, a welcome visitor to the squadron was the renowned artist, Cuthbert Orde, who drew a number of the pilots.

On 28 July, the composition of the Tangmere Wing changed. Bader continued to lead with 616 Squadron, but 145 Squadron left for a rest period, and 41 Squadron flew down from Catterick to replace them. As they settled in over the next week, few operations were flown, and it was not until 7 August that 616 was able to fly its first sweep for almost a fortnight. The operation west of Bethune was successful, and Derek Beedham and Jeff West claimed a damaged each.

During the morning of 9 August, the Tangmere Wing was tasked to provide target support for Circus 68, on their way to Gosnay. The two Westhampnett squadrons took

The CO, Billy Burton, with the Earl of Titchfield, at Westhampnett, July 1941.

off at 10.40, with Bader in the lead. Flying with him were Jeff West and 'Cocky' Dundas, with Johnnie Johnson completing the leader's 'Dogsbody' section. Billy Burton led Yellow Section and 'Buck' Casson was at the head of Blue Section. When 616 and 610 arrived over the rendezvous point at Beachy Head, there was no sign of 41 Squadron. An irritated Bader decided to press on without them. Bader had also discovered that his airspeed indicator was not working, and, although it was accepted practice that a pilot should turn back in such circumstances, Bader decided to press on.

The formation of Spitfires climbed to 28,000 feet and, as they crossed the French coast, they were warned that twenty-plus bandits were in the area. Just after another warning that more bandits had appeared, Roy Marples spotted the first of the enemy. Within minutes German fighters started to appear from above and below, and there was some confusion over their numbers and exact positions. Bader took his section down to attack some of the enemy, and Casson followed with his section. Many years later, 'Buck' Casson recalled the fight:

> I was well throttled back in the dive, as the other three had started to fall behind and I wanted to keep the flight together. I attacked from the rear, and after having a squirt at two Me 109s flying together, shot down another. The other three 'B' Flight machines were in my rear and probably one of the lads saw this. I climbed to 13,000 feet and fell in with 'Billy' Burton and three other aircraft. We chased around in a circle for some time, gaining height all the while, and more 109s were directly above us. Eventually we formed up in line abreast and set off after the Wing.

Many radio calls were made, and it was soon apparent that the squadron was involved in a major engagement. Suddenly, someone called 'Break', without giving any further instructions, and this created even greater confusion. In a conversation with the author many years later, 'Johnnie' Johnson commented that 'it was an absolute shambles with aircraft everywhere and a great risk of collision. I was being chased by a number of Me 109s and I decided to get the hell out of it and dived for the nearest patch of cloud to take refuge'. Through his headset he could still hear the fight going on above, with a constant stream of radio calls being made.

After joining up with Burton's section, Casson saw a lone Spitfire below him, apparently in trouble, so he called Burton and peeled away to assist. In the event, Burton did not hear his call.

As he approached the straggler he assumed Burton's section was behind him, and he pressed on. At that moment his aircraft was hit in the engine, and it was then that he saw that two Me 109s were behind him. With the engine overheating and running rough, he dived to low level, but more shells hit the cockpit and smashed the rudder pedal. With fuel filling the cockpit, the engine finally seized, and Casson belly-landed in a field near Marquise. The victorious Me 109 flew overhead, and the pilot, 'Ace' Hauptmann Gerhard Schopfel, noted the Spitfire's (W 3458) markings for his combat report. Casson set fire to the Spitfire's cockpit, and within minutes was arrested. Casson recorded the events of the day in his diary:

Offensive patrol over Gosnay. 616 Sqn attacked by number of Me 109 aircraft. DB had a collision with a Me 109 and baled out. I flew back with 'A' Flight, but seeing a lone Spitfire at about 1000 ft broke off to assist. My aircraft was hit by Me 109s, and so I descended to tree top height and made for the coast, but the Me 109s fired cannon shells into my engine, which seized up. I crash landed in a field on the edge of a wood near St Omer. Germans with rifles rushed out before I could escape, and I was brought before a German general.

Meanwhile, the rest of 616 were heading home. As he crossed the French coast at low level, 'Johnnie' Johnson saw a lone Me 109, which he attacked, sending it down with black smoke streaming from its tail. When he arrived back at Westhampnett, Group Captain A.B. 'Woody' Woodhall, the sector controller and Tangmere station commander, met him as other pilots started to arrive back. It was soon apparent that the engagement had been one of utter confusion. A note in Johnson's log book adequately sums up the sortie; 'More opposition than ever before. Wing Commander Bader missing. 'Buck' Casson missing'. He later added to the same page: 'In this last flight, W/C Bader shot down one Me 109 in flames and then collided with another before successfully baling out – German Intelligence. This information received 30/9/41.'

As soon as it became obvious that Bader and Casson would not be returning, 'Cocky' Dundas organised a search over the English Channel. He took Johnson, 'Nip' Heppell and Jeff West with him, and they headed for the French coast at Le Touquet where they started to sweep along the likely return route, but all they found was an empty dinghy. With their fuel getting low, Dundas had to abandon the search and he turned the formation for Hawkinge.

Both pilots were flying 'Presentation' Spitfires. Bader was flying W 3185, which had been gifted by Mr Oswald Finney, and bore the name *Lord Lloyd I*. 'Buck' Casson was flying W 3458, gifted by the Muirfield Fund, and bearing the name *Muirfield* on the engine cowling.

The loss of these two highly experienced pilots was a huge blow to the squadron. Sheffield-born 'Buck' Casson's loss was particularly poignant as he had been with the squadron since its formation. In his book *Flying Start*, 'Cocky' Dundas wrote:

> 'Buck' Casson's loss affected me very deeply, as we had been together so long. And it was terrifying as well as a desolate thing to realize that now I was the last left of the founder group; it followed, inevitably, that I must be the next to go.

Over the years there has been a great deal of speculation about what exactly happened to Douglas Bader's aircraft. Some of the best fighter pilots who knew Bader well, such as Johnson and 'Laddie' Lucas, were always convinced that a pilot of *JG 26* had shot him down, and there is evidence to support this view. As late as 1996, Lucas maintained his view, which was reinforced after he dined with Adolph Galland that year. What is clear is that as Bader dived from 24,000 feet onto a group of Me 109s, his Spitfire was hit from behind. He always maintained that, as he turned, another aircraft had collided with him, and the tail and rear fuselage of his aircraft had sheared off – an opinion he voiced until his death. He tried to bale out, but the right foot of his artificial leg became trapped under the rudder bar. Eventually he broke free and parachuted safely to the ground where he was soon captured. That evening he was the guest of Oberstleutnant Adolph Galland, the Kommodore of *JG 26*, and his pilots.

With the lack of any German evidence that a collision had taken place involving one of their aircraft, and no RAF aircraft suffering from collision damage, recent theories have speculated that Bader was shot down, and there is some evidence that Bader may have been a victim of 'friendly fire'. Sadly, and understandably, given the mass confusion in an air battle, this was not an uncommon event. However, until positive evidence becomes available, such as the recovery of the remains of Bader's Spitfire, the exact circumstances are likely to remain a mystery.

On 14 August the great news came that Bader had survived and was a prisoner. With the added news that 'Buck' Casson was also a prisoner, there was much rejoicing in the squadron. This was tempered, later in the day, when Sergeant Lawrence McKee failed to return from an offensive patrol over Boulogne. However, just as some of his predecessors had done, he managed to evade capture and, with the help of the 'Pat' escape line, crossed the Pyrenees and was back in England by December.

Through the Red Cross it was learnt that Bader needed new artificial legs. The Germans offered to give an aircraft free passage to deliver the legs, but the Air Ministry decided that they should be dropped during a routine bombing operation instead. So, on 19 August, a Blenheim of 82 Squadron, escorted by 616 Squadron's Spitfires, dropped the legs in a

Wing Commander Douglas Bader DSO, DFC, Tangmere's Wing Leader.

container over St Omer during a small-scale bombing raid. The Germans recovered the container, and Bader soon made use of his new legs by escaping from the clinic where he was being held. His freedom, however, was short lived, and he would spend much of the rest of the war in Colditz Castle.

The loss of Bader, who had led the Tangmere Wing for five hectic months, was a major blow for everyone. Johnson considered him to be the 'greatest tactician of all'. Dundas summed up the pilot's feelings with the simple statement, 'he was bloody marvellous, that's all there was to it'. He was an inspiration to the pilots, and the deeds and successes of those that flew with him speak volumes for the effect Bader had on them, and the lessons he had taught them. However, there are also some with a very different opinion, and it appears that views on Douglas Bader polarized into two distinct camps. No one doubted his aggression, determination to fight the enemy, or his bravery, but there were those who found him to be rude and his manner too self-centred. Not everyone was sorry to see his departure. Many felt that his treatment of the squadron's popular and effective commanding officer, Billy Burton, was 'shabby'. Since Bader led every sweep, Burton had few opportunities to develop his own leadership skills, unlike other squadron commanders. The loyal ex-Cranwell Sword of Honour winner attracted widespread praise for the manner in which he accepted a situation that must have been deeply frustrating for him.

Nevertheless, with Bader gone, there was a gaping hole in the leadership of the Wing. His failure to delegate and share the lead with Burton, or his other squadron commanders, left the Wing with no natural successor.

With the posting of the stalwart Roy Marples to 41 Squadron as a flight commander, during August, the character of the squadron was changing. Amongst the aircrew, only 'Cocky' Dundas remained from the old auxiliaries, and the squadron was becoming a typical RAF fighter squadron, with a mix of British, Commonwealth and Allied pilots. The ever-faithful ground crew had suffered less turmoil, and many of the originals still remained, but they were quick to appreciate that things were changing. However, they welcomed new arrivals with the traditional goodwill and friendship that is part of the way of life of South Yorkshire folk.

Amongst the new arrivals was Dennis Hill, who had arrived to work in the squadron's orderly room in April. He commented:

> By 1941 some of the original members of the squadron, mostly from South Yorkshire and Lincolnshire, had been posted away from 616 and their places taken by men from other parts of the UK, so it became a squadron with people from all over the country. As a lad from Somerset, I was accepted into the presence of the original personnel and treated as one of their own.

The loss of Bader and Casson, and the posting of Marples, created a number of changes in the squadron. Casson and Marples had been with the squadron for a very long time, and their influence across the whole spectrum of squadron life, operational, tactical, and social, allied to their very presence as apparently indestructible, had a great impact on the others. Flight Lieutenant 'Mitzi' Darling arrived as a flight commander, but within the month his former squadron reclaimed him. Alan Smith was commissioned and became a section leader.

By mid-August RAF fighter losses were mounting. Some were beginning to question the value of the offensive, including Commander-in-Chief Sholto Douglas. It was also clear that, despite the claims made in good faith by pilots, the Luftwaffe's fighter force did not appear to be on the decline.

After the 'leg operation', the squadron recommenced sweeps, but at a much less intense rate. Escorts for anti-shipping operations were flown, and convoy patrols reappeared. After losing four pilots on a sweep to Bethune, on 21 August, the long-serving 610 Squadron, under the command of Ken Holden, was finally withdrawn, on 30 August, leaving 616 as the senior squadron in the Wing. The squadron also assumed 610's role of providing top cover for the Wing.

The last day of August provided the Wing with its busiest day since the loss of Bader and Casson, and 'Trapper' Bowen shot down a Me 109 and damaged a second during a sweep to cover a circus to St Omer. On 4 September, Johnson and West combined well when the squadron intercepted eight Me 109s. Johnson selected one and took his Yellow Section into the attack. Both West and Johnson scored hits before they had to break away, and the rest of the section saw flames break out and the enemy fighter dive away. However, no one could say for certain that the 109 had been destroyed, so the two pilots claimed a shared highly probable.

In mid-September, Johnson was promoted to flight lieutenant, and made the flight commander of 'B' Flight. The following day it was announced that 'Nip' Heppell and Johnson had each been awarded the DFC, and Jeff West the DFM – the only one awarded to a member of 616. There was also a DFC for 'Buck' Casson, who was languishing in Oflag XC, near Lubeck. This latter award created a hat-trick, as all three of the original auxiliaries, Casson, Dundas and Holden, had all been awarded the DFC. The one sad feature during this brief period of celebration was the departure, on 21 September, of 'Cocky' Dundas, the last of the squadron's South Yorkshire auxiliaries. Dundas, who went on to become one of the RAF's youngest group captains, and earn two DSOs, was exhausted and in need of a rest. On leaving his beloved squadron he commented:

> When it came to the point [to leave] my inner relief at being removed from the danger of the 109s was quite swamped at the sadness of leaving 616 Squadron. There was a tumultuous farewell party and the next morning I was poured into the back cockpit of the squadron Magister and flown in a semi-moribund state to Cumberland.

The end of the 1941 summer offensive was drawing to a close, but not before the squadron achieved further success. After seeing off 'Cocky' Dundas on the 21st, 616 took off to provide an escort for Blenheims attacking Gosnay. Just after passing Le Touquet at 19,000 feet, thirty to forty Me 109Fs were engaged. Johnson led 'B' Flight into the fight, and within a few minutes had shot down two of the enemy, bringing his confirmed total to six. Alan Smith also destroyed a Me 109, and Sergeant Brooker claimed a damaged. The recently arrived Sergeant J.C. Carter was shot down ten miles south of Le Touquet, but was able to bale out of his Spitfire (AB 795) and was taken prisoner.

22 September was a sad day for the squadron. Whilst on a training flight over the sea, just south of Brighton, Pilot Officer E.H. Burton RCAF and Sergeant J.B. Slack collided. Both were lost. There was more sadness four days later when Pilot Officer R.G. Sutherland failed

to return from a sweep. His aircraft (W 3334), which had been gifted by the Blackpool Fund and carried the name *Progress I*, was hit and seen to dive to 10,000 feet, where he appeared to straighten out. His fellow pilots thought there was a chance that he would make a forced landing, but news came through that he had died. The laconic and amusing twenty-two-year-old Canadian was buried at Gamaches. All on the squadron had admired his courage after he was seriously injured in a landing accident on 2 June. After recovering he managed to return to 616, and had only recently resumed operational flying. Returning from the same sweep, Jeff West had to bale out off Bexhill, but he was soon rescued. He was flying W 3655, donated by Brigadier C.L. Lindemann, and named *Silver Grey*. West recorded what happened:

> While on a fighter sweep at altitude over northern France, I had an oxygen failure near Amiens. I lost consciousness and the Wing. On reaching lower level I regained my senses to find the cockpit full of glycol fumes, the radio gone and three 109s having a meal of me. Streaming smoke, I powered vertically to ground level and shot out to sea down the Seine estuary. I tried to nurse the engine to Beachy Head. When approaching the English coast, as the oil pressure departed, I pulled up to 800 feet and, as the flames appeared, elected for the salt and baled out, leaving Spitfire VB W 3655 at the bottom of the English Channel. Two fishermen from Bexhill rescued me.

On 1 October, the squadron flew its last sweep along the French coast between Cap Gris Nez and Boulogne. Me 109s were encountered and attacked head on, but no results were observed.

Group Captain Victor Beamish, a staff officer at Headquarters No.11 (Fighter) Group, was a regular visitor to the squadron, but on his visit at the beginning of October he brought news that 616 was to withdraw from the front line and head back to Kirton-on-

Johnson's Spitfire VB (AA 879) showing the squadron's new code, YQ.

Squadron Leader Billy
Burton DFC, OC 616
Squadron.

Lindsay for a rest. He took Billy Burton to one side and told him that it was time for a rest; Squadron Leader C.F. Gray DFC, a New Zealander with sixteen victories, would be arriving the following day to take command. Burton protested, but it was no use. Beamish was firm, and reminded Burton that he was the longest-serving officer on the squadron, during which time he had also shouldered the great burden of being in command.

Burton had proved an immensely popular CO. As 'Johnnie' Johnson commented, his job was finished. He had taken over a demoralised squadron twelve months earlier, trained them up again, and been at the head of a fighting squadron that had acquitted itself so well. With his Cranwell background, and sense of loyalty, discipline and professionalism, he had been the ideal man to resurrect the fortunes of a squadron desperately in need of firm leadership after the rigours of the Battle of Britain. He had instilled flying discipline, and created and overseen a rigorous training programme for new pilots, before leading them into battle in January 1941. Despite the presence of Bader, he had led his section on most of the squadron's major sweeps, and had flown on over sixty operations – as many

Johnnie Johnson's Spitfire carries the squadon's determination to keep 'Bader's Bus Company Still Running'.

as any other pilot. The citation for his DFC, which had just been announced, concluded with the fitting comment, 'he has been an inspiration to his squadron'. Few would disagree that Billy Burton was 616 Squadron's finest wartime commander. Tragically, as a wing commander, having added a DSO and a Bar to his DFC, he was killed in June 1943 when the passenger aircraft bringing him to England from the Middle East was shot down over the Bay of Biscay.

On 7 October, the squadron's 'high summer' of intense operations came to an end with the move to Kirton-in-Lindsay, where 'the permanent staff welcomed them back with lavish hospitality'. The ground crew travelled by train, and on the outside of the carriages leaving Kings Cross a chalked message read 'Bader's Bus Company Still Running'.

CHAPTER SIX

RODEOS, RAMRODS AND RHUBARBS

The move to Kirton-in-Lindsay brought the squadron much closer to its spiritual home of South Yorkshire, and to the homes of most of the airmen. It also meant that the Spitfire VBs were exchanged for the Mark IIs of 65 Squadron, who were moving to Westhampnett to replace 616.

Each auxiliary squadron had an honorary air commodore, and 616 was fortunate to have the Marquis of Titchfield, who had always shown the greatest interest in the activities and fortunes of the squadron. His estate was at Welbeck, near Worksop, where squadron personnel were always welcome. In their autobiographies, both 'Johnnie' Johnson and Colin Gray recall joining the Marquis for pheasant shoots, a regular activity over the coming months. Johnson commented 'those days were some of the happiest of the war years'. A comment by one of the estate workers, when asked if they would do one final beat at the end of a cold day, sums up the mutual respect and affection when he was heard to say, 'we'll beat till midnight for 616, m'lord'.

With the move north, the squadron had come under the control of 12 Group, who always provided a duty wing of Spitfires that could be sent to reinforce the squadrons in the south. On 8 November the squadron positioned at RAF West Malling, and joined up with two Canadian Spitfire squadrons, 411 and 412, to patrol near Dunkirk, providing withdrawal cover for a bomber force attacking Lille. The Canadians were heavily engaged, and, as 616 went to their aid, a swirling dogfight with the Me 109s ensued. However, some of the pilots, including Heppell and Johnson, were convinced that they had also seen a radial-engine fighter. Wing Commander D.R. Scott, the wing leader, failed to return.

Back at Kirton-in-Lindsay the pilots sat with the intelligence officer, Gibbs, and discussed and sketched their ideas of the new aircraft, and their comments were sent to air intelligence. Some weeks later, after more sightings of the new enemy aircraft, it became apparent that the RAF had made its first encounters with the redoubtable Focke Wulf 190.

Much of November and December was taken up with flying convoy patrols, scrambling against 'X' raids, and training. There had been a significant turnover in pilots, and the new arrivals, most of them nineteen and twenty year olds, built up their experience under the guidance of the remaining stalwarts. Jeff West and Alan Smith, who had recently been commissioned and awarded the DFC, left to pursue outstanding careers in the Middle

East, leaving Johnson, Heppel and Beedham as the only pilots left from the early days. Also leaving was Warrant Officer Hawthorn, the wireless NCO, who had been one of the earliest to join, in 1938, and was now on his way to Digby. The squadron also lost the long-serving adjutant, Flying Officer F.J. Walter, who had been in post since the Dunkirk days. He left to train as a pilot for non-operational duties, since he was over the age of thirty-one. During this period, Spitfire VBs replaced the squadron's ageing Mark IIs.

At this stage of the war the 'South Yorkshire' Squadron could almost have been renamed 616 (Commonwealth) Squadron, with most of the Commonwealth countries being represented by the new arrivals. In Johnson's Flight there were three Canadians, four New Zealanders, an Australian and a Rhodesian; he was one of only two Englishmen, the other being Sergeant N.G. Welch.

The New Zealander, Jeff West, captured the mood of many of the Commonwealth pilots who had joined their South Yorkshire colleagues, when he wrote in 1987:

> You will no doubt appreciate that I have a very soft spot for 616, or Six-Worn-Six, as Ken Holden would say. It was my first squadron. On looking at my log book I see I had 189 hours when posted to 616 at Tangmere in March 1941. Six hours on Masters, twenty on Spits and the rest on Tiger Moths. The encouragement and example of the others saw me survive, commissioned on the squadron and allowed to stay with the boys. It is now difficult to understand the excessive enthusiasm that made me volunteer to go to Malta in February 1942 and desert 616, where I had been so happy and been accepted and made to feel at home, despite being referred to as 'the wild colonial boy', and especially when I called the 'drome a paddock!

The CO, Squadron Leader Gray, and Flying Officer 'Huck' Murray RCAF, tried a new venture on 10 December. They set off for RAF Martlesham in Suffolk to refuel before taking off for an offensive patrol over southern Holland, their target being the distillery at Bergen Op Zoom. Unfortunately the weather deteriorated when they made landfall, thick mist coming down to 200 feet. They saw and attacked two barges drawn by a tug, and observed their cannon shells registering hits.

The New Year got off to a bad start for the squadron when Flight Sergeant M.M. Waite RCAF failed to return from a convoy patrol off Skegness. The squadron flew a number of searches to locate him but, sadly, he was never found. After ten days flying from Goxhill to test its suitability as a fighter airfield, 616 moved to Kings Cliffe, a satellite of the sector airfield at Wittering, where the famous Group Captain Basil Embry was station commander. It was also time to bid farewell to Derek Beedham, who had spent almost two years with the squadron, and had acquitted himself so well. He too left for the Middle East where he was commissioned.

The routine of convoy patrols, scrambles, and training continued. Brief detachments to reinforce the southern fighter squadrons on bomber escort operations remained a feature of the squadron's activities. The tedium was relieved for a few days when ten aircraft flew to Matlaske, on 12 February, when six aircraft escorted Whirlwind fighter-bombers seeking the German battlecruisers *Scharnhorst* and *Gneisenau* during their epic Channel dash. Nothing was seen and the squadron returned to normal routine. One unusual activity was to provide airborne escorts for captured Luftwaffe aircraft that had been

Pilots of 'B' Flight at Kings Cliffe, in January 1942. *Left to right:* Ware (NZ) (killed), Bowen (Can), Johnson, Colin Gray (CO), Bolton, Winter (Rhodesia), Strouts (Can) (KIA).

brought to Wittering for evaluation by a specialist flight. Although these aircraft carried RAF markings and serial numbers, an RAF fighter escort was an added safety measure. On 27 February, the squadron said goodbye to its CO, Colin Gray, and welcomed his successor Squadron Leader H.L.I. Brown from 609 Squadron.

There was a lack of flying during March, but this did not prevent a number of accidents happening. On the 13th Pilot Officer R. Large made a successful crash landing in the Magister after running out of fuel. The following day he returned to take off, but unfortunately hit a bullock, seriously injuring the animal and writing off the Magister. The following day Sergeant Welch hit a tree on landing, and on the 16th Pilot Officer H.R. Strouts was landing when he hit another Spitfire that was taxiing into position.

During a formation practise on 25 March, the Wing was intercepted by Typhoons, and, in the ensuing melee, another aircraft struck Sergeant C.J. Baxter's aircraft (AD 459), and he was forced to bale out at 16,000 feet. He suffered minor injuries. Sergeant A.R. Winter's aircraft was also hit, his port mainplane being damaged, but he managed to make a forced landing at Wittering.

The arrival of April brought a number of changes, and some intense action, when seven sweeps were flown over France. The squadron flew down to West Malling on 12 April to join 412 and 609 Squadrons in forming a Wing to cover a force of twelve Bostons returning from an attack on the marshalling yards at Hazebrouuck, in northern France. Little action was seen, but Pilot Officers H.R. Strouts RCAF and M. Lepel-Cointet (Free

French) failed to return. Not since the Battle of Britain had the squadron had two pilots killed on a single operation. Fighter squadrons are very close-knit units where everyone knows everyone else, so a double loss was very keenly felt, not least by the ground crew who always waited anxiously for the return of 'their' pilot. The following day, a fighter sweep was flown over Le Touquet, but on return to Kings Cliffe from Wittering, the squadron learned that Sergeant G.L. Davidson RNZAF had been killed over the airfield. Twelve Yorkshire press photographers and reporters were visiting the station to meet 616 personnel. Davidson took off and immediately started a slow roll at 100 feet, but failed to recover and crashed into a field adjoining the base. As the operations record book commented 'it was an awkward situation for the press to be there'. The young New Zealander is buried at Wittering.

Early on the 15th, another bomber escort was flown from West Malling to provide cover for bombers attacking Desvres. Johnson attacked a FW 190 at 18,000 feet, near Le Touquet. Smoke poured from the German fighter's engine, and pieces broke off the fuselage, but Johnson was only able to claim a damaged, his final success with 616. Sergeant P.C. Miller RAAF was forced to ditch his Spitfire (BL 754) in the English Channel four miles south of Dungeness. He was injured, but an air-sea rescue launch soon came to his aid.

Towards the end of April, pilots were sent to Boscombe Down to convert to the new high-altitude version of the Spitfire, the Mark VI. The aircraft, developed to meet a high-level reconnaissance threat, had a pressurised cockpit and a high altitude rated engine, the Merlin 47, with a four-bladed Rotol propeller, but the pilots did not like the 'clamped on' bubble canopy, which could not be opened in flight. The cockpit was heated, making it much more comfortable at height, but below 15,000 feet it was unbearably hot. 616's

Spitfire IIA (P 8367) maintenance.

pilots had climbed above 40,000 feet on practise flights, and the squadron continued to operate as part of 12 Group's routine operations.

Fighter pilots were renowned for their high spirits and aggression. Colleagues claimed that Pilot Officer R.G. 'Bob' Large possessed enough of both to equip a whole squadron, and he often found himself 'on the carpet' for some high-spirited misdemeanour. On 8 May he was conducting an air test in the region of the Wash. In 1990 he recorded what happened next:

> I remember well that at that time of the war there had been a number of tip-and-run raiders, usually lone Dorniers, who had been causing havoc and escaping in broken cloud. In the course of my general evolutions, I came over the top of a loop and looking down at a large fluffy white cloud when I spotted a twin-engine, twin-finned aircraft that looked like a Dornier Do 17 bomber. I was ideally placed to attack it from above and behind. Sure enough the aircraft emerged from cloud and I was closing in fast with reflector sight on and gun button on Fire. I closed in and was about to open fire when I noticed the RAF roundels on the wing and flicked the gun button to safe, but could not resist continuing the mock attack, firing only my cine-gun. After several spectacular attacks, I flew in formation with the aircraft (which was a Flamingo and nothing like a Dornier) and gave the pilot a V for Victory sign. I thought he was waving back, but later learned he was shaking his fist!
>
> I broke away, thinking nothing of it and was soon in the circuit. Imagine my surprise and amazement when, clambering out of my Spitfire, I was met by a senior intelligence officer and placed under arrest. This officer, who was unknown to me, was almost incoherent with rage, and I was taken to the operations room. To my intense dismay I learned that Lord Trenchard had been on his way to Scotland with other senior officers and, being a VIP, had to remain in radio contact with ground control. It was then revealed that after my first simulated attack as I rolled over and broke away underneath the Flamingo, my starboard wing tip took away the trailing aerial and effectively silenced his radio. The aircraft could not therefore continue its journey and had to land at North Luffenham to have the necessary repairs. Lord Trenchard's engagements for the day had to be cancelled. The future of Pilot Officer Large looked bleak.

Large was soon ordered before the station commander, Group Captain Basil Embry, where he became the recipient of a huge 'rocket', and was given seven days orderly officer duties. A few days later, Large had an altercation with a fighter control officer, and he found himself under close arrest pending a court martial. Basil Embry, himself one of the most aggressive pilots and commanders in the RAF, recognised talent and spirit and allowed Large to fly on offensive patrols 'on the understanding that you come back!'

There was an unexpected sequel to the Trenchard incident, which Bob Large relates:

> Whilst completing my period of duty as orderly officer at Wittering, I was having lunch in the mess when the station adjutant approached me and told me quite casually that Lord Trenchard wished to see me in the lounge. Since I had naturally been the subject of much leg pulling over this matter, I thought this to be another attempt to catch me out. I therefore continued my lunch at my leisure, arose from the table, poured myself a coffee and strolled quietly into the lounge. Instead of the usual crescendo of voices emanating from the bar at one end of the

room, there was a decided air of restraint, and officers were talking quietly in groups, very much on their best behaviour.

The reason was obvious. There at the end of the room was the towering figure of Lord Trenchard with the station senior officers. I paused briefly to put down my coffee and check my uniform before approaching the group. Group Captain Embry, who sighted me almost immediately, introduced me to the great man in his forthright and outspoken way, 'this is the young man who nearly killed you last week'.

'Boom' Trenchard was kindness itself. He shook my hand warmly, bought me a beer and told about a similar story that had happened to him between the wars. After a brief conversation he again shook my hand and wished me well. I could not help noticing that throughout this conversation, Boom talked exclusively to me and not to the group as a whole. Likewise, I could not fail to notice the rings on his sleeve, those of Marshal of the Royal Air Force, compared to my tiny thin stripe of pilot officer. As previously, with Basil Embry, I was privileged to see the greatness of these men at first hand and appreciate their qualities of leadership.

During the late afternoon of 25 May, the squadron had an increasingly rare call to scramble, one that provided its first combat with the new Mark VI aircraft. Green Section, of Pilot Officer C.B. Brown and Sergeant N.G. Welch, were directed to patrol over Leicester at 2,000 feet to investigate a lone aircraft. 'Johnnie' Johnson heard the aircraft start up and rushed to the squadron dispersal to find out what was happening. Minutes later, he took off with Australian Sergeant J.H. Smithson as his wingman. He soon spotted a lone aircraft and gave chase. He was unsure of its identity but held his fire. Then, as he broke away, the gunner of a Dornier Do 217 opened fire, before disappearing into cloud. Brown and Welch closed in, and Brown was able to attack and see a wisp of smoke start to steam from one of the enemy bomber's engines. As he broke away the enemy gunner's fire shattered the cockpit of his aircraft and bits of perspex hit him in the face blinding him in one eye. Despite his serious injuries, he managed to make an emergency landing at nearby North Luffenham.

Brown lost his right eye but was determined to return to operations. In due course he joined a night-fighter squadron, and many years later he retired as an air commodore, having commanded a V-bomber base and been known throughout his long RAF career as 'Cyclops' Brown.

The following day, Pilot Officer L.B. 'Tess' Ware RNZAF was killed during practise formation flying. Sergeant Welch broke away from the formation with engine trouble and made a successful forced landing on the racecourse at Market Rasen. Shortly afterwards, Ware's Spitfire (BR 172) turned away and went into a dive. His wingman, Sergeant Featherstone, followed him for a short time, but Ware's aircraft started to dive steeper, reaching such a speed that the wings broke off and the aircraft crashed and burnt out near Lincoln. He was buried with military honours at Scampton.

June could hardly have got off to a better start. On the first day of the month, almost a year after he had been shot down, 'Mac' McCairns visited the squadron, after his marvellous escape from a German prisoner of war camp. Many of the ground crew faces were familiar to him but, of his fellow pilots, only Johnson remained.

On the 3rd the squadron was fully equipped with Mark VIs, but a restriction was put in place that limited operational flying to heights above 20,000 feet, due to the excessive heat in the cockpit. Australian-born Flight Lieutenant F.A.O. Gaze DFC arrived on the 3rd to command 'A' Flight. It was to be another day starting with a flight down to West Malling for a sweep in the Boulogne area. A squadron of Me 109s was seen, but no engagements took place. On return to West Malling, it was discovered that Australian Pilot Officer P.J. Moore, of 'A' Flight, was missing. In due course it was learnt that he had been shot down off Le Touquet and was laid to rest in the Etaples Military Cemetery.

Four days after a sweep over Dunkirk, on 5 June, the squadron was thrilled to learn that 'Johnnie' Johnson had been awarded a Bar to his DFC. The final sentence of the citation that accompanied the award summed up the feelings of all the squadron: 'Flight Lieutenant Johnson is an exceptional leader and the magnificent example he sets is an inspiration to other pilots.'

June proved to be a very quiet month with no further operations. This slack period was interrupted when Sergeant W.A. Clouston RNZAF crashed into the sea, just north of Sheringham. He had gone off on a weather check and air test, and was seen carrying out aerobatics at low level just before he crashed. He had just seventeen hours experience in a Spitfire.

7 July saw the squadron move to Kenley, in the 11 Group area, to replace 485 Squadron, and the following day saw the first operation, a Channel sweep, flown in the Boulogne area. Two days later saw the end of an era with the departure of one of the squadron's greatest pilots. 'Johnnie' Johnson, who had served with 616 for almost two years, and was virtually the last of the Tangmere Wing pilots, was promoted to squadron leader and posted to command 610 Squadron. Johnson had been an inspiration to the air and ground crews, and had developed a tremendous affection for, and loyalty to, the squadron, which lasted for the rest of his life. His two ground crew, fitter LAC Fred Burton, and rigger LAC Arthur Radcliffe, were devoted to him, and he reciprocated their feelings, maintaining contact with them throughout their lives. On his last night, the whole squadron turned out to wish him well, and the party in a local pub lasted into the early hours. The following morning, Johnson left for 610 Squadron, and went on to become one of the RAF's most charismatic and successful fighter pilots.

Tony Gaze was soon into his stride as the new flight commander. During a sweep south of Abbeville, on 13 July, he probably shot down a FW 190. Five days later he was able to claim the squadron's first confirmed victory with the Spitfire VI. Together with Pilot Officer Park RAAF, he was scrambled at 08.50 to investigate a bandit, but as he approached the French coast he turned back. His combat report picks up here:

About half-way across the Channel, flying at 500 feet, I saw two aircraft, which I identified as FW 190s, flying in the opposite direction about five miles away and right down on the sea, so I turned and chased them using 14 lbs boost, and managed to close to 500 yards. The Huns were then heading towards a bank of low cloud, so I fired three short bursts of cannon at the nearest aircraft on the starboard side to try to make it turn before entering cloud. Instead, the enemy aircraft started a gradual dive toward the sea, so I dived steeply and managed to get ahead of them, 500 feet below the leader who was on the port, and I pulled up under him, giving a short burst of cannon and machine-guns, which hit him in the belly and starboard wing. The undercarriage dropped and I gave him another burst of about two seconds as he turned left diving toward the sea. The other FW 190 also turned left sharply, so I followed it

'Johnnie' Johnson with his ground crew, Arthur Radcliffe and Fred Burton, with their aircraft, the Manchester Civil Defender.

around and fired a burst seeing a cannon strike on the fuselage. My cannon then ran out, so I fired my machine-guns with no result… I called up my No.2, who had now caught up, and told him to close up and chase the Hun home while I took a cine-shot of the pilot of the first 190, who had pulled up in front of me and had baled out at 700 feet. I had fired my machine-guns as he pulled up in front of me and, as he baled out, flames poured out of the cockpit and the aircraft went straight into the sea. The pilot's parachute canopy had several large holes in it and I think he must have been wounded as he made no attempt to release himself from his parachute and was being dragged by it across the water when I left.

The wounded pilot of the FW 190, Feldwebel Klaus Oldermann of *II/JG 2*, was rescued.

The squadron was ordered to move to Great Sampford, near Saffron Walden, in Essex, on 29 July. The Spitfire VI performed best at high altitude, so it was argued that the squadron should be based further north in order to have the time to climb to their operational altitude to provide cover for the other squadrons. However, less than twenty-four hours later, this logical solution was completely abandoned when they were tasked to fly a 'ramrod' to St Omer, remaining at 500 feet until halfway across the Channel, then commencing to climb. The order to climb came late, and as the squadron passed through 20,000 feet, fifty plus FW 190s of *JG 26* bounced the formation. The next few minutes were to mark the worst reverse suffered by the squadron for almost two years.

Kenyan-born Sergeant Mike Cooper described the first few minutes of the fight:

The whole squadron was bounced by a group of 190s, one of which attacked my No.1 who went into a vertical climb. I followed firing all guns, but suddenly found that my aircraft was losing all power. There was another 190 behind me and one of its bullets had punctured the coolant radiator under my aircraft. I broke away smartly and headed for England, giving the Mayday emergency signal as I went. Soon the engine temperature was dangerously high and, fearing fire, I baled out. I followed the correct procedure of rolling the Spitfire onto its back and pushing the stick hard forward so that I was, in effect, on the outside of a circle and the negative 'g' threw me out of the aircraft. I was in mid-channel off Cap Griz Nez. As I floated down I noticed another Spitfire plunge into the sea and a parachute descending about half a mile away. Once in the water I released my parachute and set about inflating the rubber dinghy that, for fighter pilots, was part of the total parachute pack forming the seat in the aircraft.

Mike Cooper and his ground crew at readiness.

Having got safely into the dinghy I started paddling towards the other pilot whom I could see quite clearly paddling towards me. Progress was slow and long before we could join up, we were both picked up separately by two RAF Air-Sea Rescue launches. I was told I was lucky to be collected because I was paddling away from England! We were taken to Hawkinge aerodrome near Dover where, after quite a party, we were flown back to the squadron.

The other pilot rescued was Bob Large, Cooper's No.1. Large's aircraft was hit by Hauptmann Johannes Seifert, a Knight's Cross holder, but he managed to 'clobber' a FW 190 before he inverted his stricken Spitfire and baled out to join Cooper in the sea. The rest of the squadron was also at a great disadvantage following the bounce. Sergeant Donald Lee's aircraft was badly damaged and he struggled bravely back to Biggin Hill. Unfortunately, just before landing his aircraft burst into flames, and young Lee died at the controls of BR 243. Worse was to follow, and the squadron waited anxiously for the return of Pilot Office J.R. Mace. He never arrived, and was posted as missing. In due course he was reported to be a prisoner of war. It had been a black day for 616 and for Fighter Command, with seventeen Spitfires, five Hurricanes and a Typhoon destroyed, eleven pilots killed and three made prisoners. Two others managed to evade capture and eventually returned to England.

When Canadian troops and British Commandos made their 'reconnaissance in force' against the French harbour town of Dieppe, on 19 August, they were supported by the largest array of RAF aircraft yet mounted for an operation. Sixty-eight squadrons flew almost 3,000 sorties – all in just sixteen hours. 616 Squadron moved from Great Sampford to Hawkinge for the operation, and pilots came to readiness at dawn to provide top cover, taking off at 07.00 for their first patrol over Dieppe. The squadron mounted four major operations throughout the day, and some pilots flew on all four patrols. The second was to give support to 416 (RCAF) Squadron in the battle area, as troops endeavoured to withdraw. Fifty FW 190s were seen, as well as a lone bomber. The latter was attacked and destroyed by Flight Commander Tony Gaze. Four pilots each damaged a FW 190. Sergeant N.G. Welch's aircraft was damaged, but he made a successful belly landing back at base. Sergeant N.W.J. Coldrey, a Rhodesian, failed to return and was later reported as killed in action. He was buried in the cemetery at Middelkerke.

No sooner had the squadron landed than it was called into action for a third time to give top cover to a force of Hurricane bombers attacking gun batteries firing on Allied shipping. The CO, Squadron Leader Brown, was leading the squadron at 12,000 feet when a group of ten FW 190s were spotted and engaged. Bob Large had 'several squirts' at the enemy fighters, claiming a damaged, as did Pilot Officer Smithson. Flight Lieutenant J.S. Fifield's aircraft was hit, and he was forced to bale out. He took to his dinghy and was picked up from the Channel by a minesweeper, and landed at Newhaven later in the day. In the early evening, the squadron scrambled for the fourth time, this time to give cover to the last of the naval vessels as they withdrew. It had been a hectic day, and one of the most challenging for the pilots of Fighter Command.

At the end of the month, Tony Gaze was promoted to squadron leader and posted to command 64 Squadron. Flying Officer G.B. MacLachlan was promoted to replace him in command of 'A' Flight.

On 9 September the squadron had a rare opportunity to attempt a very high level interception. Pilot Officer P.J. Blanchard and Sergeant Goodyear were scrambled from Great Sampford at 15.30 and vectored east with instructions to climb to high level. Twenty miles south of Clacton they sighted a German aircraft flying south-east. Still climbing, and keeping the enemy aircraft in sight, they managed to reach 38,600 feet, over Ramsgate. The German was still 4,000 feet above them when they were ordered to return. Both pilots reported that the aircraft was a Junkers 88, but the debriefing officer thought it more likely that it was a Junkers 86P, a specialist high-altitude reconnaissance aircraft.

For the next few months, the squadron remained very active both on sweeps and escorting USAAF B-17 Flying Fortress bombers over France. On 2 October twelve 616 Squadron Spitfires took off to join Circus 221 and provide close escort to six B-17s attacking Longavesnes airfield near St Omer – Bob Large flew as White 3, with his friend, Flight Sergeant Mike Cooper, flying as White 4. As the formation was leaving the target, twelve FW 190s appeared about 6,000 feet below, and Large set up a diving attack. He caught a straggler, and started firing from 500 yards, holding a five-second burst, with the result that the enemy fighter caught fire in a steep dive. Post-war analysis indicates that Unteroffizier Hans Stoller of 2/JG 26, who managed to bale out despite being wounded, was piloting the German aircraft. Large had to break away from the engagement as other fighters threatened, and exhausted his ammunition in a head-on attack on another FW 190 before heading for the coast with Cooper, flying line abreast, and with enemy fighters giving chase. Almost immediately, a FW 190 closed in on Cooper and attacked him from below, hitting the radiator of his Spitfire. A glycol leak started almost immediately, and Cooper had to bale out at 17,000 feet, landing in the sea two miles off the French coast. As he watched his friend clamber aboard his dinghy, more FW 190s attacked Large, who, with no ammunition, had to fly hard to escape them. He noted Cooper's position, broadcast a 'Mayday' call, and raced back to Hawkinge.

On landing, his aircraft was refuelled and he immediately took off, accompanied by Flight Lieutenant J. Fifield, to re-locate Cooper – there had been insufficient time to re-arm the Spitfire. He spotted Cooper, but was almost immediately attacked by four FW 190s, which were eventually driven off by Fifield and other Spitfires of 402 (RCAF) and 416 (RCAF), which had appeared on the scene as escorts to a Walrus air-sea rescue aircraft, piloted by Flight Sergeant Tom Fletcher DFM. Large continued to orbit the dinghy as the other Spitfires kept more enemy fighters at bay. The Walrus dropped a smoke float to keep Cooper in sight. In the meantime, it had become apparent that Cooper was floating in an enemy minefield. Royal Navy patrol boats and RAF High Speed Launches sent to rescue Cooper decided it was too risky to enter the area, so Fletcher landed in the minefield, despite coming under fire from shore batteries, and taxied between the mines that were just visible on the surface. A rope was thrown to Cooper, but the Walrus rear crew were unable to get him on board, so Fletcher had to make another perilous orbit amongst the mines for a second attempt. This was successful, and with Cooper safely on board, Fletcher took off with shells splashing around him, and with Large and the other Spitfires giving top cover. Fletcher was recommended for the Victoria Cross for this gallant rescue, but this was reduced to a Bar for his DFM. The *London Gazette* issue of 3 November announced that Bob Large had been awarded an immediate DFC 'for his gallantry and forethought, which set a praiseworthy example.'

The squadron moved again on 30 October, returning to its old airfield at Westhampnett. Two days later Sergeant P.S. Smith (RNZAF) was lost. Accompanied by Sergeant J.K. Rodger, he took off at 14.15 on a convoy patrol. Fifteen minutes after take-off the weather deteriorated and they were recalled to base. Both aircraft crashed into a low hill near Ventnor on the Isle of Wight, and Smith, who was on his third operation, was killed. Rodger's aircraft hit a brick wall and he was able to make a forced landing. He escaped with concussion and slight head injuries.

During November and December, the squadron was constantly engaged in offensive sweeps and escort sorties for B-17s. Tony Gaze had returned to take over 'B' Flight from Flight Lieutenant J.S. Fifield, who had left to command 124 Squadron. On 27 November, he and Sergeant W. McKenzie (RCAF) took off on a 'rhubarb' sortie to the Dieppe area, where Gaze shot up a long goods train on an incline. The train stopped, and then ran backwards, with steam pouring from the boiler. McKenzie attacked two goods trains in Abbeville marshalling yards, seeing strikes on both engines. At the end of the month, it was announced that 616's CO, Squadron Leader H.L.I. Brown, who had just married, had been awarded the DFC.

During this busy period, some pilots, including Bob Large, flew no less than thirty-three operations, but his long tour with 616 Squadron was coming to an end. In the New Year he was posted as an instructor to the Fighter Leaders School at Aston Down, after flying continuously on operations for almost two years, during which time he flew 188 operational sorties, and was credited with two destroyed, one probable and one damaged – all achieved at a time when top cover and close escort sorties afforded less chances for the high-flying Spitfire VIs to engage the enemy. So the squadron said goodbye to one of its greatest characters and the last of the Tangmere Wing pilots. A measure of Bob Large's impact and influence on the squadron can be judged by the comments of a pilot who joined 616 after Large had left. He commented:

> When I first arrived I would sit in the crew room and the name that cropped up the most was this fellow Bob Large. He was always being mentioned in every conversation together with the antics he got up to and his aggressive and ebullient spirit. After a few days, I asked where this chap was and got the reply, 'Oh! He left a few months ago'. He obviously had made a huge impression on the other pilots but I never did meet him and often wished I had.

A few days after Bob Large's departure, it was time for more farewells when the CO, Squadron Leader Harry Brown, left to attend the RAF Staff College, and was replaced by Squadron Leader G.S.K. Haywood.

The end of 1942 saw the establishment of a pattern of operations that would last for the next eighteen months, leading up to D-Day. It was to be a period of continuous escort duty, not only for 2 Group's medium bombers, but also for the USAAF's 8th Air Force heavy bombers and the 9th Air Force medium bombers. Fighter Command had developed its concept of 'wing' operations to a very effective level, and the Wings became very adept at moving at short notice to advanced airfields for a few days, before returning to their parent airfield. For those squadrons operating in the west of England, such as 616, range became an issue. The Spitfires, designed as air defence fighters, did not have the endurance to loiter in target areas, and so long-range fuel tanks had to be carried, which sometimes inhibited manoeuvring against the ever-increasing numbers of the highly capable FW 190s of the Luftwaffe.

The New Year brought a change of location for the squadron, and on the 2nd the aircraft started flying into Ibsley, in the New Forest. There was also an influx of new pilots, including four Belgians. As with all fighter squadrons, 616 provided an element on standby for scrambles and convoy patrols, and these were to remain a regular feature of daily operations. Escort sorties were resumed later in the month when the squadron accompanied Bostons bombing Cherbourg. The 21st brought the excellent news that the ebullient, aggressive Tony Gaze had been awarded a Bar to his DFC for 'his great skill and fine fighting spirit'.

On 22 January, Flight Lieutenant P.B. Wright DFC, who had only recently arrived in 616, was returning from a sortie over France when he saw the crew of a Ventura floating in the sea after ditching their aircraft. He set up an orbit above them and, after much twisting and turning in his cockpit, he managed to free the dinghy he was sitting on and drop it to the men in the water.

Being based at Ibsley meant the squadron could get involved in operations of a longer range, usually into the western part of France and the Brest Peninsula. February was a particularly busy month escorting Venturas, Bostons and Whirlwinds to targets near Cherbourg and around Cap le Hague. The 7th saw a diversion when the squadron provided an escort for the Prime Minister's Liberator 'Commando', on his return from the Casablanca conference.

The beginning of March was dominated by one of the largest and most important tactical exercises mounted in England during the war, Exercise Spartan. One of the primary aims was to test the plans being developed for the eventual invasion of France. Medium bombers of 2 Group provided the attacking 'enemy' force, with 616 making up one of the defending squadrons. Air Marshal Sir Trafford Leigh-Mallory, the Air Officer, Commanding-in-Chief of Fighter Command, visited Ibsley and spoke with the pilots at their dispersal, stressing the importance of learning to work with the army in the field, another of the aims of the exercise.

On each day, the squadron came to readiness at dawn, and were scrambled as required. On 4 March, sixteen Typhoons 'raided' Ibsley, and one aircraft of 616 was adjudged to have been destroyed, with two damaged, and six pilots wounded and out of action. Later that day four 616 Spitfires scrambled and intercepted two Mustangs and a Typhoon south of the airfield. A later assessment of the cine-gun camera shots of this combat allowed the pilots to claim all three aircraft as destroyed.

During the afternoon, the squadron took off to rendezvous with twelve Hurricane bombers at Chilbolton. They escorted these to Charlbury, in the Cotswolds, where the Hurricanes attacked an M/T park of 50-60 vehicles. On the way to the target, Red Section attacked and destroyed a hostile Mustang, and, after leaving the target, the squadron beat up an aircraft park at Kidlington airfield near Oxford, where approximately thirty Spitfires and fifteen Mustangs were closely parked. Squadron pilots claimed twelve damaged or destroyed for the loss of three pilots and aircraft. After leaving the Hurricanes at their base, 616 met twelve Typhoon bombers with hostile markings, west of Romsey, which they attacked. The Typhoons took no evasive action and the exercise umpire assessed their losses as seven destroyed.

This major exercise continued in a similar vein until 12 March, and many lessons were learned. Then it was back to normal routine, with a sortie to escort a force of Whirlwinds to Cherbourg. By the end of the month a further six pilots had joined the squadron, and these included three Australians and two Canadians.

On 4 April, the squadron suffered its first loss for almost five months when Flying Officer P.J. Blanchard was killed when his Spitfire (BR 310) crashed after hitting a barrage balloon cable. His parents later 'adopted' the 616 in his memory, and they opened their house in London to any member of the squadron visiting the capital. The same day saw the departure of the CO, Squadron Leader G.S.K. Haywood, on health grounds. He had been a popular boss and the squadron was sorry to lose him. Squadron Leader P.W. 'Pip' Lefevre DFC, a veteran of the Norwegian and Malta campaigns, replaced him.

The following day the squadron flew to Portreath with 129 Squadron for a circus as escort cover to twelve Venturas bombing the docks at Brest. Intense, heavy flak was encountered over the target, but several bombs were seen bursting in the docks. Ten miles out to sea, on the return, still escorting the bombers, one of the Venturas ditched, and Blue Section dived on four FW 190s orbiting the crew in the sea. More enemy fighters joined in and a fierce combat took place. Sergeant H. Bailly's Spitfire was badly damaged, but he managed to struggle back. Thirty miles south of the Lizard, another Ventura ditched, and Flight Lieutenant G.B. MacLachlan detached his dinghy and threw it out to the stricken bomber crew. The squadron had to land at Predannock, but the gallant Peter Wright DFC, in BS 465, failed to return, and he is commemorated on the Runnymede Memorial.

During April the hard-working ground crew experienced great difficulty in keeping the aircraft serviceable. Only 100 of the Mark VI version had been built, and the supply of spare parts became an increasing problem. On 15 April only ten aircraft could be made available for a sweep and two of those returned early with faults. With long sea crossings in the single-engine Spitfires, aircraft had to turn back if they encountered problems. Observing the aircraft on this sweep, from the ground, was the squadron's honorary CO, Air Commodore the Marquis of Titchfield, whose enthusiasm and support for the squadron was as strong as ever.

A maximum effort was called for on the following day. The Spitfires flew down to Perranporth to refuel, and were airborne just after noon to escort twenty-four USAAF Liberators bombing Brest. Leading the squadron, for the first time was the new CO, Squadron Leader 'Pip' Lefevre. The 616 Spitfires were flying as rear escort above the Liberators, into and out of the target. Intense heavy flak at 22,000 feet over the target was encountered, and the CO's aircraft was hit and seen spinning down. He managed to bale out, with his parachute opening at 12,000 feet, and he drifted down on to a moorland area covered in gorse, where he avoided capture. After leaving the target, Yellow Section was attacked, and Sergeant T.D. 'Dixie' Dean probably destroyed a FW 190, but the twenty-one-year-old Gordon MacLachlan was shot down and killed in BS 245. His body was recovered and he was buried in the village of Plouguerneau. During his time on the squadron, MacLachlan had created an excellent impression and been appointed a flight commander. Tragedy struck the MacLachlan family again three months later when his elder brother, James, who had lost his left arm in combat, but had later returned to fly Hurricanes and Mustangs, was killed, on 31 July, having been awarded the DSO and three DFCs.

No.616 Squadron at Westhampnett in October 1942. *Standing, left to right:* Eng Off, Fowler (Can), unknown, unknown, Miller (Aus), unknown, Mackenzie (Can), Rodger, unknown, unknown, Cooper (Kenya), unknown, Smith, unknown, unknown, Joubert (FF). *Front:* Adjutant, unknown, Blanchard, Maclachlan, Earl of Titchfield, Sqn Ldr Brown (CO), Smithson (Aus), Large, McClelland (NZ), Orton.

Two days later yet another Spitfire suffered an engine failure and Sergeant S.J. Fowler was forced to ditch. He got safely into his dinghy and waited as orbiting Spitfires protected him until an ASR launch arrived to pick him up.

April had been a busy month, and it had taken its toll, even on the more experienced members of the squadron. The new CO had lasted only a few days, and both flight commanders had been lost. However, some weeks later, it was learned that 'Pip' Lefevre was, in true 616 fashion, on his way home having avoided capture. In the meantime, 616 gained a CO and a flight commander of great experience, when the Malta veteran, Squadron Leader P.B. 'Laddie' Lucas DFC, arrived to take command on the 20th, and a few days later Flight Lieutenant L.W. Watts, another veteran of the Malta Siege, joined as a flight commander. Morale was also given a boost when Sergeant Philip Wareing visited the squadron on 29 April. He had been shot down during the Battle of Britain, to become a POW, but had since managed a dramatic escape to Sweden, a feat that earned him the DCM.

The pattern of operations was much the same during the summer months with the squadron mounting a number of sweeps and escort missions. Scrambles became less frequent but the need to maintain a pair of aircraft on standby remained. Convoy patrols, thought by the pilots to be the most boring of all operations, and therefore reserved for the newer pilots, still featured regularly. The excitement and feeling of making a worthwhile contribution to the war effort came from the sweeps, which sometimes provided an opportunity to attack the enemy. These operations could vary. For example, on 21 May, four aircraft took off in the morning to fly an offensive patrol over Cherbourg and the Channel Islands. They were sent to intercept a high-level enemy patrol that had been spotted over the Channel Islands, but they met with no luck. In the late evening, a second patrol flew at nought feet to the same area, but also saw nothing. During the same day, a convoy patrol was flown, and two pairs of aircraft were scrambled to investigate contacts, but they too had no luck. A busy, and typical day that produced no positive results.

In contrast, the squadron diarist described 23 May as having 'bags of action today!' The CO, 'Laddie' Lucas, led a formation of eight aircraft of 616 flying in the anti-flak role, and eight of 129 Squadron, acting as escorts, to provide support for four Whirlwind bombers in an attack against a small convoy off Guernsey. The convoy was just about to enter St Peter Port when 616, now ahead of them, attacked three small ships with cannons and machine-guns. Strikes on the wheelhouse of one, and on the waterline of another, were observed, and a small battery of machine-guns was silenced on a third. The Whirlwinds scored hits on two of the ships and the pilots spoke highly of the effectiveness of 616. The Spitfire flown by Les Watts was hit in the rear fuselage by flak and the rudder controls were put out of action. He flew back to base using the rudder trim, and made a skilful landing despite the aircraft being badly damaged.

The opportunity for air-to-air combat rarely occurred, but on 29 May two aircraft finally managed to engage enemy fighters. Pilot Officer Joubert des Ouches, and the Belgian, Sergeant J.L.J. Croquet of 'B' Flight, took off on a high-level patrol between Portland Bill and the Needles. They had been airborne for an hour when they were given a vector of 340 degrees. Two FW 190s were seen, and both Spitfire pilots jettisoned their fuel tanks to close in, taking one aircraft each. Joubert opened fire at 600 yards and the enemy dived to sea level, followed by the Spitfire, but it gradually drew away and disappeared in the mist. Croquet opened fire at 300 yards, and saw a piece fall from the FW 190, which also dived to sea level. Croquet pursued it to the French coast, where he had to abandon the chase. Both pilots claimed a damaged.

The summer months followed the same pattern, with frequent short-duration detachments to airfields such as Exeter, Manston and Martlesham Heath. Eight large-scale escort operations were flown in June, with a similar number in July and August. As usual, these formed only a part of the overall flying effort of the squadron, but they were the most notable features. Unfortunately, the squadron lost a pilot on 15 June, during an attack against a convoy of minesweepers off Guernsey. The Spitfire (BR 319) of the very experienced twenty-three-year-old New Zealander, Flying Officer R.J. Sim, was hit by flak. He pulled away from the formation and was last seen at 300 feet gliding towards the sea with a dead propeller and his aircraft on fire. He made no attempt to bale out, and is commemorated on the Runnymede memorial.

A different task came the squadron's way when aircraft were provided to escort the King to RAF Northolt. As the King stepped down from his aircraft the Spitfires flew past and dipped their wings in salute.

No.616 Squadron at Ibsley in the summer of 1944. Seated in the centre (right of dog) is the CO, Watts, flanked by his two flight commanders, Dennis Barry and Mike Graves.

Another aircraft was lost on 29 June, during an escort sortie for eighty USAAF Fortresses, when Flying Officer A. Drew, who had joined 616 three weeks earlier, was forced to bale out. As he jettisoned his fuel tanks, one hit the tailplane of his Spitfire (BR 314). He was able to retain some control and headed back towards the English coast, but, despite his best efforts, had to abandon the aircraft over Waterlooville.

'Laddie' Lucas left on 4 July, on promotion to be wing commander at Coltishall. Leslie 'Watty' Watts, one of the flight commanders, was promoted to take command – a very popular choice with all the squadron air and ground crew. A week later came the excellent news that the former CO, 'Pip' Lefevre, had reached Gibraltar, adding to the growing list of 616 Squadron pilots who were downed on enemy territory but managed to keep out of the clutches of the Germans. On return, he took command of a Typhoon squadron, where he increased his score of enemy aircraft destroyed. Tragically, whilst leading a sweep over Brest in February 1944, his aircraft was hit by flak and he was seen to bale out, but did not survive.

The end of July saw the squadron constantly on the move, first deployment to Bradwell Bay in Essex to provide escort cover for Venturas bombing the coke ovens at Zeebrugge. On landing they moved to Coltishall in Norfolk, and later that evening escorted twelve Mitchells bombing Schipol airfield in Holland. Just after crossing the Dutch coast, a section of Me 109s was seen, and some of the squadron gave chase, firing at long range, but no results were seen. The following morning 616 took off from Coltishall to give close escort to twelve Bostons bombing the Fokker aircraft factory at Amsterdam. When leaving the Dutch coast they spotted an enemy convoy of some twenty ships, escorted by a deadly *Sperrbrecher* flak ship, which was reported to the controller.

After these three successful operations the squadron returned to Ibsley at noon on 28 July, but three hours later left for Tangmere. At 18.15 they took off to escort eighteen USAAF Marauders who, according to the squadron diary, 'did not seem to know the form'. After making a rendezvous over Beachy Head, they set off on the wrong heading. They proceeded towards Belgium (their target was in northern France) and as they were about to coast in, the Ibsley wing leader, Wing Commander E.H. Thomas DSO, DFC, called the controller, who had no choice but to call the formation back and abandon the operation.

The following day, the squadron set off for Martlesham Heath for an operation to escort a large force of Marauders attacking Woensdrecht airfield in Holland. The US bombers did not drop their bombs, but the squadron met eight FW 190s. The CO claimed one damaged, and three other pilots opened fire with no result. All the Spitfires returned safely, but a Marauder, and a Spitfire of 66 Squadron, failed to return.

Before the end of the month, the squadron flew to Manston to provide another escort. So, over a period of a few days, the squadron had flown operations from no less than five different airfields, not including their own at Ibsley. With hindsight, one has to wonder at the efficiency and economy of employing the fighter squadrons in this way. At the time, Fighter Command had over fifty day fighter squadrons available, and the airborne threat to the country had virtually disappeared. Escorting the bomber force was obviously an important task, but a great deal of time and effort was wasted with squadrons constantly flying from one airfield to another. It also presented major problems for the squadron's engineering and support staffs.

During this hectic period came the excellent news that the CO, Squadron Leader Leslie Watts, had been awarded the DFC for 'invariably displaying courage, skill and tenacity'.

Squadron Leader L. Watts DFC,
OC 616 Squadron.

Ten more escorts and sweeps were flown during August. On the 16th, a beautiful day without a cloud in the sky, the squadron diarist noted that 'at 10.30 the squadron took off from Ibsley for a change', tasked to escort twelve Venturas attacking Bernay airfield near Le Havre. It was the first operation led by the new Ibsley wing leader, Wing Commander J.E. Charles DFC and Bar. Mike Cooper was leading Blue Section. After climbing into his usual aircraft he discovered an oxygen leak and had to hastily transfer to another (BR 987), taking off at 11.00. Many years later he recalled what happened:

The visibility was terrific and we could see the French coast long before we reached mid-Channel. We crossed the coast at 23,000 feet just north of Le Havre. Our controller told us over the radio-telephone that there were no Huns about. As we turned south from Le Havre I could see the bomb bursts on Bernay. I had just opened my throttle to keep in position on the outside of the turn when I felt my engine run rough. I noticed there was no flak about so did not worry. We were about 60 kilometres inland when I noticed the roughness increase. While turning westward, back towards the coast, the roughness became steadily worse. I called up my squadron leader and reported the vibration and he sent another flight to cover me. Oil pressure had dropped right off the clock and the glycol temperature was way above the safety level. I called again saying that I had 'had it' and was heading back into France. (All escape lectures stressed that the coast area was to be avoided because it was the defended zone.) Right from the onset of things I had one thought, to evade capture and return to England.

As I turned inland the boys wished me well. 'Leave the French girls alone', 'Good luck', 'See you in the Chez Moi' (a 'dive' in London frequented by squadron members when in the area). The last I heard was 'cut the natter' from the CO, and I was on my own heading southeast at 17,000 feet. The engine was very hot but still working. Nonetheless I made up my mind to bale out. I wasn't scared, I had done it twice before, so why not again. Looking below I saw a town to my left and open country to my right. At this time the engine had become extremely hot and was beginning to smoke. I was afraid of fire and made the immediate decision to bale out. I detached my oxygen tube and wireless plug, undid my straps with the speed at 200 mph and height 9,000 feet. Barrel rolling onto my back, bracing myself and pushing the stick fully forward, I managed to eject myself from the kite and was falling through the air. As I turned over and over I pulled the rip chord. Instantly I was jerked upright, all was quiet and still.

So began an adventure that would last until December, when Mike Cooper became the seventh member of 616 Squadron to return from enemy-occupied territory. Ironically, the day after Cooper went missing, 'Pip' Lefevre paid a visit to the squadron and gave advice on how to avoid capture when he related his experiences of travelling through France and Spain to Gibraltar.

The end of August proved costly for the squadron. Returning from an early morning shipping reconnaissance, Flight Sergeant R.T.Wright (RAAF) was forced to ditch his Spitfire (BS 115) four miles off the coast, south of Christchurch. He was soon picked up by the Air-Sea Rescue service. On the 31st, the squadron mounted twenty-one sorties throughout the day, on an air-sea rescue operation, searching for a Mustang pilot twenty miles north of the Ile de Batz, off the Brittany coast. At 15.00 Wing Commander J.E. Charles, the wing leader, took off from Exeter with eight aircraft on the final search. Eight FW 190s bounced the formation and a fierce engagement developed. The wing leader and Flight Sergeant F.W.

Rutherford destroyed one each, and a third was damaged. However, it was a costly operation, as Flight Sergeant Ron McKillop, who was on his third search of the day, and twenty-year-old Sergeant Paul Shale, were shot down, in addition to a Spitfire of 276 Squadron. All three pilots were lost and are commemorated on the Runnymede Memorial.

There was much rejoicing as September started and the first of the Spitfire VIIs arrived, to start replacing the increasingly unserviceable Mark VIs, which had always been unpopular with both the pilots and the engine fitters. With its two-speed, two-staged, supercharged Merlin 61 engine and retractable tail wheel, the Mark VII had a better performance and was 40mph faster.

The first operation with the new Spitfire was a scramble, on 14 September, and within the week all the old Mark VIs had left. The majority of the squadron's activities during September had been to the Brest Peninsula, and in order to increase the range, the aircraft had operated from Predannack, in Cornwall. On the 17th, the squadron moved to Exeter, where the routine of convoy patrols, scrambles and the occasional escort sortie continued. On 5 November, the engine of Sergeant W. Gordon's Spitfire VII (MB 929) failed as he was returning from a patrol, and he ditched ten miles south-west of Portland. A long search failed to find him, and he was posted missing. The twenty-one year old is commemorated on the Runnymede Memorial.

On 21 October, twenty-year-old Pilot Officer Alan F. Smith (RAAF) and one of the squadron NCOs, Flight Sergeant E.R Cole, visited Ibsley in the squadron Tiger Moth (DE 481). Just after taking off for the return to Exeter, the aircraft crashed near Ringwood and both men were killed.

The squadron was withdrawn from operations on 16 November, and left for a two-week Armament Practise Camp at Fairwood Common, where the pilots completed a concentrated period of gunnery training.

Escort operations were resumed again on 2 December, and the following day Flight Sergeant F.W. Rutherford, who had been with the squadron for a number of months, was returning in poor weather from escorting a VIP aircraft when he crashed, attempting to land at Exeter. He died of his injuries later in the day. By the end of the month, the squadron was fully equipped with eighteen Spitfire VIIs.

The first three weeks of January 1944 were very quiet, with few operations other than the routine weather reconnaissance flights, usually flown by a pair of aircraft towards the Cherbourg area. Two fighter sweeps were flown on the 4th and 5th, the first to the Pointe de Barfleur / Cap de la Hague area, and the other to Launion. These sweeps of eight aircraft, cruising at 22,000 feet, were most notable for their lack of action, and the NTR (nothing to report) in the remarks column of the squadron operations record book accurately summed up events. Finally, on the 21st, a major operation was mounted, with thirteen aircraft being deployed to Kenley to take part in an 11 Group sweep over France.

'Ramrod' sorties were to become a feature of the squadron's operations during the first part of 1944. The sweep of the 21st passed over the Cambrai area, but, as had become increasingly common, brought no response from the Luftwaffe. On the return trip, Flying Officer A.K. Dolton called that he had fuel problems and would be unable to make it back to England. He elected to turn back inland before baling out, but was almost immediately attacked by FW 190s of *JG26* and shot down. He did manage to bale out, but was soon captured, and spent the rest of the war in a POW camp.

Later in the month, the squadron welcomed back Mike Cooper, who had evaded capture and, after a desperately difficult crossing of the Pyrenees, in atrocious weather, managed to get to Gibraltar. After a rest, he went off on a gunnery course and rejoined the squadron. Cooper probably had more adventures than any other pilot to serve with 616. He was forced to bale out three times, twice landing in the sea to be rescued, the first time by a high-speed launch, and on the second by a Walrus, from the middle of a minefield. Soon after his ordeal of escaping through France to Spain, he was wounded in air combat and grounded for three months, before returning to 616 to become one of the first to convert to the Meteor jet.

A quiet January was followed by a very hectic February, with offensive sweeps, scrambles and escort missions. For the first week, most operational sorties were flown from Ford, near Chichester, and included big operations over France. Two were 'ramrods', and three involved escorting USAAF bombers to targets in the Pas de Calais region. The last of the escort missions, on the 6th, took US Liberators to Le Martin at the unusually low height of 10,000 feet, well within range of the German flak gunners.

For the next two weeks it was back to the routine of a sector fighter squadron – long periods of readiness, and the occasional scramble. However, the month ended as it had begun, with the squadron deploying in strength to Ford, Tangmere and Martlesham Heath. On the 24th and 25th USAAF Marauders attacking St Trond airfield needed an escort.

Almost since the end of the Tangmere days, 616 had a great mix of nationalities, and the period leading up to D-Day was no exception. In addition to Australians, Canadians and New Zealanders from the Commonwealth, Belgium and France were also well represented. Notably, the squadron had, once again, a South Yorkshireman amongst its pilots. Sheffield-born Flight Lieutenant D.A. Barry came from 504 Squadron as an experienced fighter pilot, and by the spring of 1944 he had been made a flight commander. In due course, he was to become one of 616's longest-serving pilots.

Little of note happened in the first two weeks of March. On the 17th packing commenced, in preparation for a move to West Malling. It was a very sad day for the squadron because the ground crew were not going to accompany the pilots, destined instead for Bolt Head. In a fighter squadron, perhaps more than any other unit, the relationship between pilots, tradesmen and support personnel was extremely close, and there were few events, operational, social or welfare, that did not come to the attention of everyone. This created a unique bond, and so it was a great wrench to have to say goodbye. The occasion did at least provide an excuse for an excellent party. At 11.00 the following day, the Spitfires took off for West Malling, and later that afternoon one section established a patrol over Dungeness. Patrols and scrambles became a daily occurrence.

The weather was poor during the afternoon of 1 April, when two aircraft were scrambled. Shortly afterwards, the Spitfire (MD 116) of Australian Flight Sergeant D.E. Johnston crashed near Tangmere, and he was killed. Three days later, Red Section was scrambled and vectored towards Lille where two FW 190s were sighted on a nearby airfield. Pilot Officer G.L. Nowell DFM and Bar led the pair down to strafe the two enemy aircraft, but the two 616 Squadron pilots made no claim.

The squadron was kept busy over the next two weeks, but no interceptions were made. However, on the 21st there was some success. Black Section was scrambled at 11.40 and vectored towards Cherbourg where the pair, led by the recently commissioned Pilot

Dennis Barry.

Officer J.C. Clerc, saw a FW 190 landing at Maupertas airfield. Clerc came astern of the aircraft and opened fire at 300 yards, and the FW 190 blew up. As the two Spitfires coasted out, Clerc's aircraft was hit by anti-aircraft fire, but he was able to return safely. The following day, another squadron Spitfire was hit over Cherbourg, and this time the pilot, Warrant Officer D.P. Kelly (RAAF), was wounded in the left eye by shrapnel. Almost blinded, Kelly called up his leader, who came alongside and instructed him to start turning for base. Gareth Nowell then coaxed him back across the Channel, giving instructions all the way, until they arrived at West Malling, where he talked Kelly down to a safe landing. A fellow pilot described it as 'a wonderful example of skill, comradeship and confidence between pilots'. After a few weeks treatment, Des Kelly returned to the squadron.

On the 24th, after just six weeks at West Malling, the squadron was once again on the move, this time to Fairwood Common in South Wales. The constant moving around of fighter squadrons is difficult to understand, and one must question the value of giving pilots a few weeks to become familiar with flying from one airfield, and the type of operations peculiar to that area, only for them to be moved to a completely different area and have to become familiar with a new area of operations. However, on this occasion, the move was probably justified, considering the momentous event that would follow in a few weeks. The first few days on the Gower Peninsula were spent on local-area-familiarisation sorties, and on the 30th, the first operation was flown from the new airfield. Eight aircraft headed for the Lizard, where they joined up to escort Fleet Air Arm Avengers on a shipping strike off Ushant.

At the beginning of May the squadron started to fly 'stopper patrols' over the Channel, and up to twenty missions a day were flown. Flying above 20,000 feet, the task was to prevent enemy aircraft making hit and run attacks on south-west England, and also to intercept any reconnaissance aircraft that might be trying to gain intelligence on activities at the various ports where invasion forces were gathering. The squadron's efforts during this period were recognised by higher authorities, and a signal was received from Air Defence, Great Britain's command headquarters, that 'the efficient patrols kept up by the squadron, which deterred any enemy aircraft from reaching the SW coast, were greatly appreciated'.

Whilst at Fairwood Common, news came that the squadron would soon be re-equipping with a new aircraft. The pilots were hoping it would be the Griffon-engine Spitfire XIV, but the arrival of a twin-engine Oxford suggested otherwise. Only the CO and the flight commanders knew what type of aircraft it would be. Mike Cooper had previously flown the Oxford, and he was tasked to give every pilot two hours practise at flying a twin-engine aircraft – a new experience for most of them.

The squadron had hardly settled in when another order to move came, and, on 16 May, boxes were packed again and the aircraft flew to Culmhead, near Exeter, before the ground crew left by train, under the supervision of the squadron's engineering officer, Flying Officer Ellis. The weather was poor, and the squadron diarist commented:

> Another busy day, this time unpacking and generally getting dispersal comfortable. Both Flights in one dispersal. Weather very cold and rain showers. After the warmth of the Gower Peninsula everybody complained of cold – we are now 865 feet above sea level.

With the move to Culmhead came a new task, one that all the pilots would become very familiar with over the coming weeks. On 22 May, Dennis Barry, the flight commander of 'A' Flight, led four aircraft on a rhubarb mission to shoot up any trains or military objectives in the Avranches-Rennes-Lamballe area. A train was found in the Folligny rail yards and the four pilots attacked. The Spitfire of the very popular Flight Sergeant G.E. Prouting was hit by flak from an armoured train and he crashed in flames just outside the village. He was buried in the local cemetery at Equilly.

Another rhubarb was flown on the following day led by the other flight commander, Flight Lieutenant Mike Graves DFC. They returned two hours later, having 'bagged' two trains, a staff car and two lorries. Later that afternoon, Dennis Barry led twelve aircraft giving cover to a force of Mitchells bombing Dinard Airfield.

Over the next few days the squadron was constantly in action flying rhubarbs over northern France, shipping reconnaissance sorties and providing escorts for the medium bombers. At this stage, of course, the pilots were still not aware that D-Day was imminent, but it was obvious that 'something was on', as pilot Flight Sergeant Bob George commented.

There was much rejoicing on the 27th when it was announced that the squadron's very popular Free Frenchman, Jean Clerc, had been awarded the Croix de Guerre with Palme.

In the days leading up to the Invasion of France, the squadron was working at maximum effort with its Spitfires. In addition to rhubarbs, convoy patrols and high-level sweeps were flown; all crucial sorties to prepare for the invasion. The key targets in North France involved transportation. Eight aircraft, led by Dennis Barry, flew on 1 June, and claimed eight locomotives, six rail wagons, a lorry and a gun post. Barry's aircraft was hit by flak and, after landing, his ground crew found a piece of shrapnel embedded in the rear fuselage. He used it as a lucky charm, and it went with him on all future sorties.

By 4 June, the weather had deteriorated, but the twelve available pilots flew many sorties, culminating in eight flying to Exeter, to be ready for 'first light' patrols the following day. Take-off was at 05.45, and all aircraft landed back at Culmhead after an uneventful patrol. After further patrols, the squadron was placed at 'readiness' at 13.00, with a section at cockpit readiness. Two hours later came the message 'all personnel confined to camp until further notice.'

The squadron operations record book captures the mood of 6 June:

> It has begun. The Allied Armies land in France. Everybody anxious for news (and excited). Convoy patrols were made by seven aircraft off Portland Bill and Start Point. Pilots returned with stories of the Channel swarming with ships of all sizes, and the skies darkened with aircraft. One section made an Air-Sea Rescue patrol for a Liberator reported down near Start Point. At 20.30 hours eight aircraft, led by S/L Watts DFC took off on Operation Rodeo, sweeping the Brest Peninsula. The squadron returned with a 'bag' of 2 locomotives and 4 military trains. Some opposition from flak but no casualties or damage. The day ended with the news that the Allied Forces had established themselves on the beaches between Cherbourg and Le Havre.

With the land forces pouring ashore in Normandy, the pattern of operations settled into a routine for the squadron. Each day a large section headed for France to carry out rhubarbs, and the tally of locomotives, motor transports etc. increased. In addition, patrols were maintained, and cover was given to the huge armada of ships crossing the Channel with men and supplies. 7 June was a particularly busy day. Eight aircraft took off at first light, to attack transport targets inland of the beachhead, when two locomotives and an army truck were destroyed. Flight Lieutenant G.N. Hobson's aircraft was hit by flak, but he managed to limp back to base. Later that morning, the CO led another rhubarb in which two more locomotives and two lorries were added to the squadron's score. Five more vehicles were attacked near Plamet and a radar station received the Spitfire's attention. Flying Officer J. Cleland added to his amusement by firing at numerous power lines and pylons. To finish this busy day, Culmhead's wing leader, Wing Commander P. Brothers DFC and Bar, led a sortie to the Brest Peninsula to attack trains, but they had to content themselves with five military vehicles instead. During the day, three patrols had also been flown off Portland. At the end of this busy day, the squadron diarist commented 'everybody "top line" but tired out'.

On 9 June, the squadron flew its first 'Beachhead Patrol' – an event 'every squadron pilot wanted to take part in'. The purpose of these crucial sorties was to ensure that the Luftwaffe did not interfere with the landings, as the bridgehead was developed and expanded. Twelve aircraft took off at 18.20, and patrolled between Trouville and Barfleur, two miles off the beach. No opposition was encountered, but the pilots were able to watch as naval ships shelled targets miles inland.

10 June was another busy day. After some uneventful patrols off Portland and Start Point, the CO took off at 10.00, leading eight aircraft on 10 Group rhubarb 275. The operations record book captured the action:

> Operation was made according to plan, covering Rennes/Lamballe area. No opposition from flak or aircraft. S/L Watts hit a locomotive near Londeau and one lorry on the Rennes road. Other claims were one truck (F/L Graves DFC), one truck at Lamballe and another at Querdillac. One locomotive (F/O Rodger) near Plougenast where Sgt Allen attacked a hutted camp. Lorries were attacked by F/L Cleland and W/O George, together with lock gates and high-tension cables. On the way back F/L Graves had engine trouble and was forced to 'ditch' 40 miles south of Start Point. Seeing F/L Graves in difficulty, F/L Cleland jettisoned his hood and prepared to throw out his dinghy, however it was seen to be unnecessary as F/L Graves finally got into his own dinghy. He was eventually brought to an ASR base by Walrus aircraft. He was taken to Royal Naval Hospital Plymouth with head and leg injuries. All wish him well and hope he will be back on the squadron soon.

After a quiet day, there was more action on the 12th. After six uneventful patrols during the morning, the squadron was tasked to fly in a Culmhead Wing operation led by Wing Commander Pete Brothers. The object of the operation (Rodeo 169) was to shoot up enemy aircraft reported to have moved to the airfields at Le Mans and Laval. The squadron acted as top cover, while the Spitfires of 131 Squadron attacked Le Mans. The roles were reversed over Laval Airfield. Flight Lieutenant G.A. Harrison and Flying Officer J.K. Rodger attacked a Me 109, and as Rodger opened fire, Harrison broke away and was seen to be flying towards another enemy aircraft. Rodger saw the wing tip of Harrison's Spitfire (MD 121) tear off the tail of the enemy before flying on. The Me 109 pilot baled out, his aircraft dived into the ground and exploded. A few second later, Harrison's propeller was seen to stop, and he was heard to say that he was preparing to bale out when his aircraft dived into the ground from 1,000 feet. No one saw the final moments, as dogfights had broken out. Warrant Officer R.A. Hart (RAAF) shot down an Me 109 near the airfield, and Jack Cleland claimed two FW 190s, both seen to crash. Other pilots turned their attention to four FW 190s, parked on the airfield. Strikes were seen on all the aircraft, and two were left burning. Cleland's aircraft had been hit by flak, and he headed for base with other pilots providing an escort. However, the engine of his Spitfire (MB 768) finally failed twelve miles south of the coast, and he baled out. He was soon picked up by an ASR launch, and he was returned to the squadron later that day. Sadly, Geoffrey Harrison, a very popular and much-liked member of 616, did not return. He was buried at Le Pellerine Cemetery.

15 June saw some of the squadron landing on French soil for the first time. Four aircraft, led by Jack Cleland, took off at 17.12 in good weather. After crossing the coast the four attacked motor transport, railway wagons, coaches and a convoy of trucks. The formation was so busy that fuel ran low, so they diverted to one of the new landing grounds in the beachhead area. They were refuelled at the American strip at Grandcamp, where the Frenchman, Jean Clerc, managed to 'discover' an oil leak in his engine, forcing him to remain behind as his three companions returned to Culmhead. He managed to ensure the unserviceability took two days to rectify, and on his return was soon giving a full account

of conditions in Normandy, and relating the great welcome he had received from the Americans and his fellow Frenchmen. Another making a welcome return to the squadron was Des Kelly, who had recovered from his eye injury.

The squadron's successes of the recent days were recognised when the Commander-in-Chief, Air Marshal Sir Roderic Hill, wrote to congratulate the entire unit for their fine performance, particularly over Le Mans and Laval.

For a few days, the Culmhead Wing turned its attention to shipping in the Gulf of St Malo and off the Cherbourg Peninsula. Bad weather forced a formation to turn back on 19 June, and the returning aircraft were twenty-five miles south of Start Part when Warrant Officer R.A. Hart called up to say his engine was cutting out. In attempting to gain height to bale out, his aircraft (MD 133) stalled and crashed. The other three aircraft orbited the scene in order for the radar station to gain a fix of the position. They searched until a shortage of fuel forced them to return to base. All that was seen was a patch of oil on the surface. The Australian, Bob Hart, is remembered on the Runnymede Memorial.

Another new task fell to the squadron on 22 June. The Wing positioned at Ford, near Chichester. Ten aircraft took off at 14.55, to escort twenty Lancasters bombing the huge V-1 storage site at Wizernes. Two days later, the squadron flew down to Tangmere, before escorting a force of Lancasters and Halifaxes bombing V-I sites in the Pas de Calais.

The end of June brought poor weather, and this temporary halt to operations was much needed by both the air and ground crews. It had been one of the most intensive periods of operations in the squadron's history. In addition to a very wide variety of operations over the English Channel, the beachhead and over northern France, the squadron had been sending a steady stream of pilots to Farnborough. The 'new' aircraft to re-equip the squadron turned out to be the Gloster Meteor jet fighter, Britain's first jet fighter. After a few sorties, the pilots returned to the squadron to continue flying operations on the Spitfire VIIs.

29 June was a sad day: it saw the loss of twenty-year-old Sergeant Vic Allen, in tragic circumstances. He took off in poor weather, and headed for Herefordshire, where his parents lived. He flew low over the village of Hope-over-Dinmore and commenced to pull up into a barrel roll but failed to recover and dived into the ground – an accident witnessed by his parents. The young sergeant was buried in the local churchyard.

Early July saw the squadron flying more sorties over France. On the 7th, eight aircraft attacked a long line of rail goods wagons and a signal box. Warrant Officer Bob George became separated from the formation, owing to radio trouble, but by the time he rejoined the formation he had successfully attacked a staff car, two lorries, and a troop-transporter south of Laval. Opposition from Luftwaffe fighters was becoming less common, and it was soon clear that the Allies had gained air superiority. However, the deadly flak was still in evidence, particularly near the railway systems, and on special wagons on goods trains.

Flak very nearly got Mike Cooper on 11 July. Twelve aircraft had taken off for the Le Mans – Tours area, where they attacked two trains. Cooper was leading a section of six aircraft when he attacked a steam train. The six aircraft were immediately enveloped in a hail of anti-aircraft fire, Cooper's aircraft was hit and he was injured in the right foot. He was forced to return, and Flight Lieutenant A.G.P. Jennings escorted him home. They saw two FW 190s very close by, but chose not to engage them. Cooper managed to land safely, and was taken to the RAF hospital at Wroughton. He would return to 616 later.

Pilots are briefed for a sweep over Normandy.

By mid-July, many of the pilots had flown the Meteor, and sufficient aircraft were becoming available to equip a Flight in the squadron. This coincided with the beginning of the V-1 threat to London, and the jet was seen as one answer to countering this sinister and effective new 'terror weapon'. 616 was moved to Manston, in Kent, to join the war against the 'Divers'.

CHAPTER SEVEN

THE JET AGE

The distinction of being the first jet squadron in the history of the Royal Air Force, and the only Allied squadron to operate jets during the Second World War, fell to 616 Squadron, one of the last of the Royal Auxiliary Air Force Squadrons to form. There has been much speculation over why one of the RAF's youngest squadrons should have this unique honour and the reasons have never been fully explained. It has been claimed that Squadron Leader Ken Holden, a former flight commander of the squadron, who was serving in the plans division of Fighter Command at the time, cheekily nominated 616 and, to his great surprise, was never challenged.

No.616 Squadron had been in existence for a mere six years when the squadron commander, Squadron Leader Leslie Watts DFC, was informed, in April 1944, that his squadron was to re-equip with the new 'secret' aircraft. Together with Flying Officer Mike Cooper, one of the squadron's most experienced pilots, Watts left for Farnborough on 26 May. There they discovered that their new 'secret' fighter was to be the Meteor jet, powered by Rolls-Royce Welland engines.

The following morning the two pilots arrived at the dispersal to find two prototype Meteor F1s (EE 213 and EE 214) being prepared for flight. Mike Cooper explained what happened next:

> The CO and I were introduced to Wing Commander Willie Wilson, the CO of the experimental flight, at his caravan. He was most pleasant and easy going. He handed each of us a sheet of paper on which was typed 'pilot's notes', which explained how to start up and fly the aircraft. We were each led to one of the two aircraft and climbed into the cockpit and studied the notes. After completing the study we reported back to the Wing Commander who asked 'any problems?' We said no, to which he replied 'then fly the bloody things.' The CO took EE 214 and I flew EE 213, and we experienced very little trouble. We each had two flights that day, and a further two on the following day. We believed we were the first two squadron pilots, as opposed to test pilots, to fly the Meteor.

Indeed they were. After three flights each, they were sufficiently confident to fly around in formation; possibly the first jet formation flying in the RAF. Watts and Cooper remained at Farnborough flying the Meteors each day, returning to the squadron's new base at

Meteor F.1 (EE 227).

Culmhead on 5 June, just in time to fly their Spitfires on a dawn D-Day beachhead patrol. During their absence a twin-engine Oxford (V 3328) had been delivered to the squadron to allow the remaining pilots to practise asymmetric flying.

Whilst the squadron continued to fly their Spitfires at an intensive rate, in support of the Normandy landings, pilots were withdrawn in groups of five, to begin the conversion to the Meteors, which were carried out initially at Farnborough. The post of squadron commander was upgraded to wing commander, and former Battle of Britain pilot, Wing Commander Andrew McDowell DFM and Bar, led the first group of five, which included a Canadian and a Frenchman. Watts was made a flight commander in the squadron. A few days later, the other flight commander, newly promoted Dennis Barry, led the second group. He recorded his first impressions of jet-flying:

The news that 616 Squadron was to become the first Allied unit to operate jet aircraft was very welcome; we were extremely pleased and excited and felt very privileged to be chosen to operate this unique type of aircraft. After an introduction to the aircraft we were briefed for our first flights. We clustered round the cockpit as the Wing Commander [Wilson] went through the drills, explaining the instruments and the aircraft's flying characteristics. Next we were told we could take off on our first familiarisation flights. This conversion briefing seemed rather sparse, especially as there were very few Meteors available. However, we felt confident, if a little over-awed, at the prospect of being chosen to fly such a novel aircraft and the honour accorded to 616.

As I taxied out to the end of the Farnborough runway in Meteor I EE 214, I ran through the drill as briefed by the Wing Commander and then I positioned the aircraft ready for take off. I held the throttles forward, giving maximum power, while holding on the brakes, then released them and the jet slowly accelerated down the runway. There was no swing and I held the stick level until 80mph was indicated, then I eased back and lifted off the runway at 120mph. With the wheels coming up, I climbed away while retracting the flaps. The rate of climb was poor at 500 feet a minute. The aircraft was quiet with no engine noise and the visibility was good with no long nose like the Spitfire. The Meteor felt heavy on the controls compared to the Spitfire and especially when full of fuel. After a forty-minute flight it was time to land remembering that by 600 feet we had to decide to carry on ahead because of the limited power for an overshoot once we were below the decision height. After landing successfully I returned to my colleagues satisfied with the aircraft except for the lack of power.

After their first flight the pilots carried out a further four flights. Another of the early pilots to convert to the Meteor was Warrant Officer Bob George, and he recorded five flights over a three-day period, practising single-engine flying and approaches on the third sortie. After this short conversion the pilots returned to the squadron as fully qualified jet pilots!

The squadron arrived at Manston on 21 July, and a few hours later the first two Meteors, the non-operational EE 213 and 214, arrived. Their arrival caused a great deal

YEAR 19.4.4...		AIRCRAFT		PILOT, OR 1ST PILOT	2ND PILOT, PUPIL OR PASSENGER	DUTY (INCLUDING RESULTS AND REMARKS)
MONTH	DATE	Type	No.			
						CATFOSS — KIRTON LINDSEY — CULMHEAD
—	—	—	—	—	—	—— TOTALS BROUGHT FORWARD
JUNE	21	DOMINI		G/C HAWTREY	SELF	CATFOSS — KIRTON LINDSEY
	22	DOMINI		G/C HAWTREY	"	KIRTON LINDSEY — HENDON.
	24	OXFORD	HM 950	F/LT ENDERSEY	"	CIRCUITS + BUMPS.
	25	SPITFIRE VII	V	SELF	—	AIR TEST
	26	"	P	"	—	AIR TEST
	27	"	W	"	—	RANGER
	29	OXFORD	HM 950	F/O MILLER	SELF	CULMHEAD TO FARNBOROUGH
	30	METEOR I	EE 214	SELF	—	EXPERIENCE ON TYPE
	30	"	EE 214	"	—	LOCAL FLYING
	30	"	EE 214	"	—	LOCAL FLYING
					SUMMARY FOR JUNE	C.G.S. SPIT. II MASTER II
				S/LDR	UNIT 616 Sqdn	SPITFIRE VII
		O/C 616 Sqdn.			DATE 30/6/44	METEOR I
					SIGNATURE gg Kistruck	OXFORD.
JULY	1	METEOR I	EE 213	SELF	—	LOCAL FLYING
	4	"	EE 213	"	—	LOCAL + ONE ENGINE APPROACH
	4	OXFORD	L H637	F/O MILLER	SELF	FARNBOROUGH TO CULMHEAD
	5	SPITFIRE VII	MD 105.	SELF	—	RANGER — LOIRE VALLEY. RETURNED WEATHER
	6	"	MD 178	"	—	RANGER — PARIS AREA. LANDED TANGMERE
	6	"	MD 178	"	—	FROM TANGMERE
	8	"	MD 178	"	—	SHIPPING RECCO — ST. PETER PORT ST. HELIER — GRANVILLE - ST. MALO.

GRAND TOTAL [Cols. (1) to (10)]　　　　TOTALS CARRIED FORWARD
....9.1.1....Hrs.....1.0.......Mins.

Entry in Flight Lieutenant Kistruck's log book showing his conversion to and first flights in the Meteor after just two training sorties in an Oxford.

of excitement and interest, and both aircraft were soon under cover in the hangar and under close guard. The following day, Captain Harold Balfour MC, MP, the Parliamentary Under-Secretary of State for Air, visited the squadron, and McDowell thrilled the visitor and station personnel with a flying display in the Meteor. Five operational aircraft arrived the following day, and the Meteor Flight was established. The honour of being the RAF's first operational jet pilots fell to Wing Commander McDowell, Squadron Leader L.W. Watts, Flight Lieutenant Mike Cooper, Flying Officers T.D. 'Dixie' Dean, J.K. Rodger and W. 'Mac' McKenzie (Canadian), Pilot Officer J.C. Clerc and Warrant Officer G.M. Wilkes.

The squadron remained fully operational, with two Flights of Spitfires, but a concentrated period to convert the remaining pilots to the jet commenced immediately. Within a week this programme was complete, and on 27 July, one Flight was declared operational on the Meteor. A few days later the squadron intelligence officer captured the mood of the squadron, entering in the record book the unique line: 'Today the Meteors go into operation. History is made! The first British jet propelled aircraft flies in defence of Britain against the flying bomb.' The privilege of flying the RAF's first operation in a jet aircraft fell to the Canadian Flying Officer W.H. 'Mac' McKenzie, who took off at 14.30 for an uneventful patrol near Ashford.

After a number of similar patrols on the first day of jet operations, 'Watty' Watts closed in on a Diver, and was ready to register the squadron's first success when his cannons jammed. Shortly afterwards, Flying Officer T.D. 'Dixie' Dean was about to open fire when control instructed him to abort, as he was entering a balloon defended area.

The sight of the Meteor over the south-east of England in the first few days of August created numerous, potentially serious misidentifications. Flying Officer Ian Wilson was returning from a patrol when two Spitfires attacked his Meteor. They opened fire on his aircraft causing serious damage to the elevators, and he had to make an emergency landing using the tail-plane trim only; an excellent piece of flying with just a few hours experience on the new jet. Anti-aircraft gunners also had trouble identifying the Meteors, as former Gunner Ron Foord recalls:

> Control told us that there was a fast target approaching at 3,000 feet. I had seen a Meteor a few days earlier but before I could shout a warning the guns started to fire. No-one noticed that it had two engines and was much bigger than a V-1, they thought it was a German aircraft. The pilot gave a remarkable display of the aircraft's manoeuvrability and every other gun opened up on it as it took evasive action and escaped. The next day we received a message from A.A. Command that said 'A Meteor aircraft will be patrolling the Thames Estuary at noon for identification purposes only – Repeat, identification purposes only.

By the beginning of August, eight Meteors had been delivered to the squadron, in addition to the two prototypes, and the aircraft was still the centre of attraction, bringing many visitors to the hangar. Patrols were flown between Ashford and Robertsbridge, usually lasting about forty-five minutes, and over the next few days squadron pilots made many more sightings, but problems with the cannons continued to frustrate them. On the 3rd, Mike Graves was convinced he was about to achieve the Meteor's first success when a Mustang impeded him and he had to break away. Finally, on 4 August, the squadron achieved its first success. At 16.16 'Dixie' Dean was flying at 4,500 feet, under the control of Biggin Hill (Kingsley 11), when he spotted a flying bomb near Tonbridge and dived in pursuit. At 450mph he soon caught the Diver, and attacked from dead astern, but his four 20mm cannons jammed as he tried to open fire. He accelerated and flew level alongside the bomb, manoeuvring his wing tip a few inches under the wing of the flying bomb so that, as he banked away, he sent the bomb diving to destruction four miles south of Tonbridge. The modest 'Dixie' Dean made it all sound very straightforward:

> I half expected the guns to jam because several other pilots had that difficulty before me. I also knew that any sudden movement would upset the V-1 and so, when my guns failed, I already had a good idea what I should do, so I just followed on in and tipped it up. When I got back to base at Manston I found there was a small dent in my wing tip where I had hit the bomb. This was the only damage to the aircraft, which was serviceable again within a few hours.

Within minutes of this first success, Flying Officer J.K. Rodger achieved a more conventional 'kill' when he shot down a flying bomb near Tenterden after two bursts of two seconds with his cannons. These initial successes were soon followed by others, and the Diver score started to mount. On 7 August the cannons in 'Dixie' Dean's aircraft worked perfectly, and he brought down his second V-1. He intercepted the Diver near Robertsbridge, at 1,000 feet. Flying at 400mph, he engaged at 700 yards, and closed to 500 yards, firing all his cannon. The Diver went down in a shallow dive and, shortly after Dean landed back at Manston, the Royal Observer Corps confirmed that it had crashed.

At 13.00 the Rt Hon Sir Archibald Sinclair Bt.PC, CMG, MP, Secretary of State for Air, visited the squadron and met all the pilots. He was keen and interested to hear first-hand news from the pilots. During the visit, Rodger and McKenzie were scrambled for a Diver patrol, and this offered an excellent opportunity to show off the Meteor.

On 10 August, six patrols were made, and twelve pilots scrambled under Kingsley 11 Control. During the afternoon, 'Dixie' Dean completed a hat-trick when he shot down a V-1 near Ashford with two short bursts. His No.2, Flying Officer H.J. Moon, saw the Diver sent spinning to earth. Pilot Officer Jordan arrived to take charge of the squadron armoury, and was immediately immersed with the armourers in trying to resolve the cannon problem.

During this period of increased operational activity by the Meteor Flight, the Spitfire Flight, under Dennis Barry, was employed mainly on weather reconnaissance flights and shipping sweeps. The weather flights flew over Belgium and the length of the French coast from Cherbourg to Ostend, as well as extending their cover as far as Amsterdam. During this period the Spitfires were leaving at a steady rate, and by 14 August the last of them had gone, and 616 became an all-Meteor squadron, equipped with fourteen of the original twenty Meteor F.1s.

The pioneers were:

CO: Wing Commander A. McDowell DFM and Bar

A Flight	**B Flight**
Sqn Ldr L. W Watts DFC	Sqn Ldr D.A. Barry
Flt Lt M.A. Graves DFC	Flt Lt R.C. Gosling
Flt Lt A.G.P. Jennings	Flt Lt T.G. Clegg
Fg Off J.K. Rodger	Fg Off M. Mullenders (Belgium)
Fg Off M.H.F. Cooper (Kenya)	Fg Off J.P. Kistruck
Fg Off H.J. Moon	Fg Off J. Ritch RCAF
Fg Off T.D. Dean	Fg Off G.N. Hobson
Fg Off H. Miller	Fg Off J.N. McKay
Fg Off W.H. McKenzie (RCAF)	Plt Off I.T. Wilson
Plt Off A. Stodhart	Plt Off K.C. Ridley DFM
Plt Off J.C. Clerc (France)	WO D.S. Kelly (Australia)
WO G. Wilkes	WO R. George
Flt Sgt B. Cartmel	WO S. Woodacre
Flt Sgt R.C.H. Easy	Flt Sgt E.E. Epps
Flt Sgt P. Watts	Flt Sgt D.A. Gregg
Flt Sgt F.G. Packer	Flt Sgt G. Amor

Adjutant:	Flt Lt E.P. Howell
Intelligence Officer:	Fg Off C.K. Doughton
Engineering Officer:	Fg Off Ellis
Armament Officer:	Plt Off Jordan
Equipment Officer:	Fg Off K. Holland
Signals Officer:	Fg Off A.E. Henshall
Medical Officer:	Flt Lt R.M. Mason

The cannons continued to cause problems, and were the cause of a tragic accident on 17 August. A Meteor (EE 225) was returning after completing a patrol in the late afternoon, when it turned into a dispersal area. As the engines were shutting down, the cannons accidentally discharged, damaging another Meteor (EE 224) and injuring four armourers and a Rolls-Royce representative. Corporal W.M. Harding was seriously injured and rushed to the local hospital, before being taken to King Edwards Chest Hospital at Midhurst, where he died, on the 25th.

The squadron started to use High Halden, a temporary airfield seven miles south-west of Ashford, as an advanced landing ground, and two aircraft and a small servicing party were positioned there each day. The RAF, and 616 Squadron, suffered its first jet loss on 15 August, when Flight Sergeant D.A. Gregg was killed. He took off from Manston (in EE 226) in the late afternoon to fly to High Halden to take up his readiness duty. Apparently he was unable to find the small airstrip, and so attempted to land at a forward airstrip

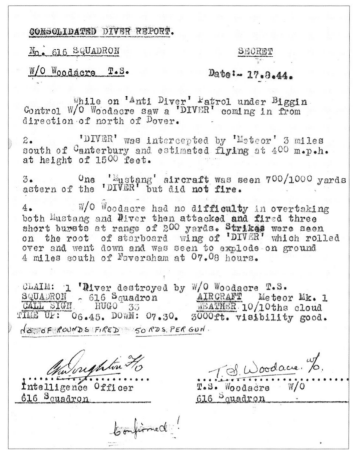

CONSOLIDATED DIVER REPORT.

No. 616 SQUADRON   SECRET

W/O Woodacre T.S.   Date:- 17.8.44.

          While on 'Anti Diver' Patrol under Biggin
Control W/O Woodacre saw a 'DIVER' coming in from
direction of north of Dover.

2.   'DIVER' was intercepted by 'Meteor' 3 miles
south of Canterbury and estimated flying at 400 m.p.h.
at height of 1500 feet.

3.   One 'Mustang' aircraft was seen 700/1000 yards
astern of the 'DIVER' but did not fire.

4.   W/O Woodacre had no difficulty in overtaking
both Mustang and Diver then attacked and fired three
short bursts at range of 200 yards. Strikes were seen
on the root of starboard wing of 'DIVER' which rolled
over and went down and was seen to explode on ground
4 miles south of Faversham at 07.08 hours.

CLAIM: 1 Diver destroyed by W/O Woodacre T.S.
SQUADRON - 616 Squadron   AIRCRAFT   Meteor Mk. 1
CALL SIGN   HUGO 35   WEATHER 10/10ths cloud
TIME UP: 06.45. DOWN: 07.30. 3000ft. visibility good.
No. OF ROUNDS FIRED   50 RDS. PER GUN.

Intelligence Officer   T.S. Woodacre   W/O
616 Squadron   616 Squadron

                    confirmed !

Warrant Officer Sid Woodacre's combat report after destroying a V-1 flying bomb.

at Great Chart, near Ashford, and crashed. The twenty-one-year-old pilot was buried in Nottingham.

The following day was a busy one, and the squadron achieved two more successes against the V-1s when 'Mac' McKenzie used the 'wing-tip method' to topple a bomb near Maidstone, and 616's Belgian pilot, Flying Officer 'Pru' Mullenders, shot one down near Ashford. The CO saw strikes on two V-1s he attacked, but had to break away on each occasion as he entered the balloon barrage, and so was unable to see the results of his attacks.

The squadron accounted for three more bombs on the 17th, one each for Warrant Officer Sid Woodacre, Flight Sergeant Sam Easy and the Canadian Flying Officer Jack Ritch. Sid Woodacre recalls his success:

Control warned me that there was a fast contact south of Canterbury at 1,500 feet, and I soon spotted it because there was a Mustang about a thousand yards behind it but not getting any closer. I passed it doing over 400mph and caught up with the flying bomb. We had been warned not to fly directly behind the bomb because the slipstream would slow us down a bit. Instead we had to approach to one side and close behind at 200 yards before opening fire. I fired three short bursts at the starboard wing root and it rolled over and blew up on the ground. I could feel the blast rock my aircraft. It was very straightforward and easy. The target was flying straight and level and didn't shoot back, what more could a fighter pilot want?

Further successes followed on the 19th, when Flight Sergeant P. Watts shot a bomb down, and Flying Officer Hobson shared one with a Tempest pilot. Ten days later he shared another with Flight Sergeant Eddie Epps. On 29 August 616 Squadron scored its last victory against the V-1 when Flying Officer Hugh Miller shot one down near Sittingbourne, bringing the squadron's total to thirteen. Earlier in the day, the CO was forced to crash-land three miles south of Manston, and his aircraft (EE 222) was badly damaged. The squadron continued to fly Diver patrols, but the recent capture of the launching sites in the Pas de Calais area had greatly reduced the number of flying bombs launched against London.

With the reduced action following the demise of the V-1s, 616 Squadron spent much of the time gaining experience of jet operations, flying in formation and demonstrating the new aircraft. During September, six pilots each week attended a Rolls-Royce engine course at a factory in the north of England. At the end of the month the press were cleared to disclose that jet-propelled aircraft were now being employed with success against the flying bomb.

A particularly important detachment of four aircraft was mounted in early October to the USAAF airfield at Debden. The heavy bombers of the US 8th Air Force had suffered serious losses to the Luftwaffe, and the appearance of the Messerschmitt Me 262 jet fighter had created an increased problem. Wing Commander McDowell flew up to Debden for preliminary discussions, and a training plan was organised with Brigadier General Jesse Auton, the commanding general. The exercise was planned to evaluate the combat capabilities of enemy jet fighters, and to determine defensive and offensive tactics for the bombers and their fighter escorts. The 2nd Bombardment Group was to provide B-24 Liberators, escorted by P-47 Thunderbolts and P-51 Mustangs.

The Meteors, flown by the CO, Dennis Barry, Flight Lieutenant Gosling and Pilot Officer Stodhart, positioned at Debden on 9 October. The following day a mixed formation of 120 bombers, in four boxes, joined up with their fighter escort over Peterborough, before setting off for the Essex coast. The Meteors, flying at 450mph, made a number of attacks, and were able to get out of range before being intercepted. Even in a dogfight, the Meteor performed well as long as the speed was kept high. During the debrief, Lieutenant Colonel Kinnard, who had led the fighter escort, commented: 'I saw the jets come in across the top of the bombers, but before I could turn into them they had passed through and gone.' Throughout the week, a series of tactical trials continued, and by the end the USAAF fighter pilots had begun to devise tactics to combat the jet threat. The debriefs were described as being 'of inestimable value'. There were also unexpected benefits for 616. One aircraft suffered a collapsed undercarriage, and another had an engine burn out, giving the squadron's servicing party valuable experience in how to service and maintain their aircraft in the field. This was to prove of great value in the coming months, as the Meteors began operating from a succession of European airfields.

Throughout November and December, the Meteors were in regular demand by RAF and USAAF bomber squadrons, for tactical training. Many fighter affiliation exercises and formation practises were flown, and pilot's practised cine air-to-air gunnery.

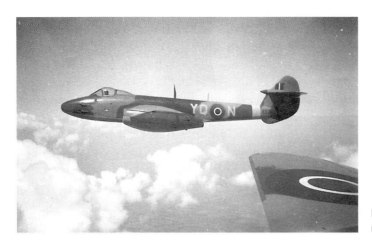

Meteor F.3 (EE 249) with the
modified cockpit canopy.

On 16 December, Colonel Clark, from USAAF Headquarters, London, visited the
squadron, and later that day flew a Meteor on a familiarisation flight. He carried out
a second flight two days later. Perhaps he was the first USAAF combat pilot to fly an
operational jet?

During December, the squadron started receiving Meteor F.3s, but the initial batch was
powered by the Welland engine, due to the slow delivery of the more powerful Rolls-
Royce Derwent engine. The first two aircraft arrived on 18 December. The CO and Sam
Easy flew to Moreton Vallence, near Gloucester, to collect EE 231 and EE 232, returning
later in the afternoon. Three more on the 24th, and two on the 28th, followed these. The
Mark 3 differed in few aspects from the Mark 1, with a new streamlined cockpit hood
being the most significant feature. From the sixteenth production example onwards, the
Mark 3 was re-engined with the new Rolls-Royce Derwent engine of 2,000lb static
thrust. This did bring a big improvement in performance, and the Meteor gained an extra
83mph at altitude.

In the 1945 New Year's honours list, it was announced that the long-serving and
adventurous Mike Cooper had been awarded a Mention in Despatches. By mid-January
all the Meteor F.1s had been exchanged for the F.3 version, and the squadron transferred to
84 Group of the Second Tactical Air Force and moved to Colerne, in readiness for a move
to the Continent. Dakotas arrived on the 28th to start transporting the advance party of
fifty ground crew, commanded by the squadron's long-serving engineering officer, Flight
Lieutenant Ellis, and equipment, to Melsbroek (B-58), near Brussels. The first four aircraft,
led by Dennis Barry, flew into the airfield on 4 February; making 616's jets the first of the
Allies' to operate from mainland Europe. The initial ground party had been very busy, and
they had everything prepared for the arrival of the first aircraft, which were immediately
painted white, as Dennis Barry explained:

> Our aircraft were painted white and we flew over Allied lines at appointed times so that our
> troops could become accustomed to the sight of the Meteors and so not fire on them in
> mistake for the Me 262 jets that were being increasingly used in ground attack missions.

Amongst the first pilots to arrive at Melsbroek was the squadron's long-serving Belgian pilot 'Pru' Mullenders. The winter of 1945 was one of the worst on record, and the Meteors were virtually grounded in early February, but a number of flights were made to familiarise local anti-aircraft gunners and pilots of other units with the Meteor. The squadron Oxford aircraft (X 7292) came in for much use as a communications aircraft, as well as being used to ferry pilots to and from Colerne. Also, the squadron had retained one Spitfire V, as a 'hack', and this was used on regular shuttle flights between England and Belgium.

Meanwhile, the rest of the squadron moved to Andrew's Field in East Anglia on 28 February, and in March returned to anti-Diver patrols. Flying bombs had reappeared, now being air-launched from Heinkel 111 bombers flying over the North Sea.

Back in Belgium, the squadron was restricted to flying over Allied territory, much to the frustration of the pilots, who saw no action. On 29 February, the BBC announced in a news bulletin 'British jet fighters – Meteors – were in action against the Luftwaffe'. The BBC's reference to the Meteors led to widespread publicity in the national newspapers the following day.

Local training flights continued for most of March. On 26 March, Dennis Barry moved his flight to Gilze-Rijen (B-77), in Holland, and Flight Lieutenant Ellis took the advance party of sixty ground crew. A large road convoy of thirty-two vehicles, with 185 NCOs and airmen under command of Flight Lieutenant E.P. Howell, the squadron adjutant, and the squadron's intelligence officer, Flying Officer C.K. Doughton, left England on the 27th, arriving at Gilze Rijen in the early hours of the 30th. Two days later, no less than seventeen new Meteors followed, and for the first time in a number of months, the whole squadron was reunited. From 3 April, two aircraft were permanently on standby by the runway, and at 16.50 two red flares were fired from flying control, and the first Allied jet scrambled from the European theatre of operations, when Mike Cooper and 'Dixie' Dean headed to patrol over Brussels at 15,000 feet, where they intercepted two friendlies, before returning to base.

Meteor F.3 (EE 239) taxis at B-58 Melsbroek, Belgium, with the all-white finish applied briefly for identification purposes.

Flying Officer 'Dixie' Dean achieved the squadron's first success against the V-1 when he tipped one over with his wing tip.

More scrambles occurred over the next few days, but no contacts with the enemy were made. It also became clear that not all Allied ground gunners had paid attention during the numerous 'identification' flights earlier, as the Meteors came under fire from friendly gunners at Nijmegan and Eindhoven.

The war was drawing to an inevitable close, and in mid-April the Meteors were cleared to operate over enemy territory. The white-painted aircraft were returned to Colerne, the others all having arrived in the standard camouflage scheme. On 13 April, ten aircraft left for Kluis (B-91), near Nijmegen, and landed on the single 1,500-yard steel-planking runway. Two aircraft were placed on immediate readiness, with the rest of the Meteors assigned to ground attack sorties. The following day the CO briefed all pilots on the squadron's new task, that of armed reconnaissance. With an operational area in western Holland bounded by Utrecht–Amsterdam–Lieden–Wagingen, the Meteors were tasked to attack any road and rail traffic in the area. The first rhubarb was flown on 16 April, but no traffic was seen and there was only light flak.

The first success fell to Mike Cooper on the following day when he strafed and destroyed an enemy truck, and other successes quickly followed, with other trucks and armoured vehicles being attacked. Over the following days, over twenty sorties were launched each day, and numerous ground targets were attacked. The squadron was soon on the move again, and on 20 April 616 was based on German soil for the first time, at Quakenbruck

(B-109), having joined 122 Wing of 83 Group. The CO led an attack against Nordholz airfield on the 24th, and considerable success was achieved. The squadron operations record book describes the action vividly:

> Fine with cloud at 3,000 feet. The Squadron briefed for armed recce of area and to 'beat up' Nordholz Airfield a few miles south of Cuxhaven. First section of four was led by W/Cdr A. McDowell DFM. Flying out of the sun at 8,000 feet the CO led the section down to attack – result, 1 Ju 88 damaged on the ground and 1 M/T to the CO. Two railway petrol tankers and airfield buildings to F/O I.T. Wilson, 12 railway carriages were strafed by F/O H.J. Moon who also silenced a gun post with one long burst. No doubt many of the Luftwaffe were keen to see the first British jet! F/Lt T.G. Clegg found a large truck full of troops on the airfield and diving in low gave them all a fine head on view. Unfortunately for the troops all four cannons were blazing away. F/O Wilson did a fine job coming back to base on one engine. Another section led by S/Ldr L.W. Watts DFC flew to Nordholz in the afternoon with F/Lt J.K. Rodger and F/Lt G.N. Hobson. S/Ldr Watts claimed one M/T and 1 airfield building while F/Lt Rodger attacked a flak post. Intense flak from Nordholz and as one pilot said, 'I could have put my wheels down and taxied across'. However, no injuries were reported although 2 aircraft received slight damage.

With the Allied armies advancing at such a pace, 616 was on the move again on the 25th, this time to Fassberg (B-152).

Tragedy struck on 29 April when the long-serving flight commander, Squadron Leader L.W. Watts DFC, and Flight Sergeant B. Cartmel, took off for a reconnaissance sortie at 14.45. They failed to return, and information was received through a radio control centre that Spitfire pilots heard Watts calling Cartmel to come closer as he was going into cloud. Shortly afterwards they saw a large explosion in the air. Both pilots were killed instantly. Watts had been an immensely popular and efficient flight commander who had served with the squadron for a long period, and his loss was a huge blow to 616, coming so close to the end of hostilities. He and Brian Cartmel were buried in Becklingen War Cemetery. Watts was replaced by the very experienced Squadron Leader Tony Gaze DFC and Bar, who was returning to 616 for a second tour. At the same time, Wing Commander W.E. 'Smokey' Schrader DFC took over as the new squadron commander.

The last two weeks of the war provided a great deal of activity, with most attacks directed at German Army units as they retreated towards Schleswig Holstein and the Danish border. The formation leader attacked the leading vehicles of a convoy, which created a blockage for those following, making them an easier target for the pilots. On 2 May over twenty vehicles were destroyed, and almost a hundred were damaged. The following day saw further successes as the new CO, with Flight Lieutenant Tony Jennings as his No.2, made a surprise attack against the airfield at Schonberg. Mike Cooper recalls the sortie:

> The CO and Tony Jennings strafed the airfield and destroyed two Heinkel 111s, two Junkers 87s and a Messerschmitt Me 109. On the return to base, Tony saw and attacked a Feisler Storch and he told us how the pilot of the Storch repeatedly and skilfully countered his attacks by turning towards him as he reached firing range so he was unable to get into a good position. As the Meteor turned the Storch landed and the pilot and a second person got out

and ran away. Tony destroyed the aircraft but made no attempt to kill the pilot; he was a brave and skilful man.

This proved to be the last opportunity for the Meteors of 616 Squadron to fight the enemy in the air. The squadron moved to Luneburg (B-156) on the 3rd. The next day was a busy and successful one, with more rail and road traffic being destroyed. Wing Commander Schrader ran out of fuel at 8,000 feet, but managed a successful dead-stick landing back at base. At 17.00 a message arrived grounding all aircraft. Hostilities in Northern Germany had ceased, before the Meteor could be pitted against a jet aircraft of the Luftwaffe. The war was over, and the squadron moved to its last base at Lubeck (B-158), the farthest east of the Allied advance. Lubeck was a permanent Luftwaffe airfield, and had been one of the Luftwaffe's Me 262 jet fighter bases. Although it had been bombed, several of the buildings and stores were undamaged, and the living quarters were good and much appreciated by all the men after many weeks of living in rough conditions.

The end of the war gave them an opportunity to relax. Some flying continued in order to display a presence to the local population, but air and ground crews were able to take advantage of captured German equipment. Not surprisingly, most people found it difficult to adjust to the new situation, and Mike Cooper captured the mood when he wrote:

> For a long time we had been in daily danger of losing our lives but now, suddenly, we found that no danger existed; the war was over, we had survived, we had won, we were the victors. No one stopped us from doing what we liked, but we did not know what we wanted to do. So we set about doing everything except molesting the German population. There has probably never been, before or since, such a situation as we found ourselves in. Our attitude towards the German people was confused. We had no hatred towards individuals but were incensed by the reports of the atrocities and terrible conditions in the concentration and extermination camps. Thus we were completely indifferent to the fate of, and certainly not sympathetic for, members of the German armed forces.

Spread around Lubeck and other local airfields were numerous serviceable Luftwaffe aircraft. Tony Gaze was particularly adept at spotting them, and after one airborne reconnaissance, set off to an adjacent airfield to commandeer a Siebel 204 light transport craft, which he then flew back to Lubeck where it became the squadron's air taxi for a period. Included amongst its other sorties were a few which involved taking airmen to see the damage to Hamburg. It was also put to excellent use as a communications aircraft when the squadron started preparations for an air display at Copenhagen. Gaze also found a brand new FW 190, which he flew back to Lubeck to have RAF roundels painted on it, and a number of the pilots had a chance to compare its capabilities against those of the Spitfire. The CO found two Me 262s, and he and Flight Lieutenant R.C. Gosling, a former test pilot, collected them, but, on landing at Lubeck, the nose wheel of 'Smokey' Schrader's aircraft collapsed and he narrowly escaped as the aircraft caught fire.

Much of the time at Lubeck was spent on a concentrated training programme for various victory fly-pasts, the most important one being by aircraft of 84 Group, at Kastrup airfield, on the outskirts of Copenhagen. Parties of ground crew had been making numerous visits to Copenhagen throughout June in order to service the aircraft during the many rehearsals. Others went to Frankfurt where, on 9 June, a formation of twelve Meteors, led by the CO, took part in a victory fly-past attended by the Soviet commander, Marshal Zhukov.

During the month, a second Bar was added to Tony Gaze's DFC. The British Empire Medal was awarded to Flight Sergeant W. Young, along with a Mention in Despatches for 'Dixie' Dean, Jock Rodger and Ian Wilson.

The award of a BEM to Bill Young was particularly noteworthy, since it was awarded specifically for his work with jet engines. He arrived on the squadron at the same time as the Meteors appeared. He had gained considerable experience on the jet engine, and the citation concluded:

Above: Meteors taxi out for take-off at the Copenhagen Victory Air Display, June 1945.

Opposite: Ground crew pose with a captured, and serviceable, Focke Wulf 190.

He has spared neither time nor effort in instructing all ranks of his Unit in the theory and maintenance work connected with the art of jet propulsion. Without doubt, this airman's efforts contributed materially to the present high standard of operational efficiency of No.616 Squadron.

After more rehearsals at Copenhagen, the day finally arrived for the show, organised to raise money for the families of children who had been accidentally killed when bombs from a Mosquito hit their school during a raid on the nearby Gestapo headquarters. On 1 July, in the presence of Queen Ingrid, a formation of five squadrons of Spitfires opened the show.

Item 5 of the show was 'a low-level flypast by 12 Meteors of 616 Squadron', which was led by Dennis Barry. Tony Gaze followed with 'a superb solo aerobatic display', and Sid Woodacre 'made a spectacular high-speed pass low over the huge crowd of spectators'. The show ended in a rainstorm, but this did not appear to dampen the ardour of the 150,000 Danes who attended. The next day the squadron returned to Lubeck, and Dennis Barry reported: 'The local population was well informed of our departure since I was able to look up at the spire of the City Hall as I led a formation of twelve aircraft over the city.'

Back at Lubeck, leisurely life continued, and at the end of July it was announced that Dennis Barry had been awarded the Croix de Guerre. Many on the squadron felt that it should have been the DFC, but the event was still celebrated in an appropriate manner when it was 'christened in the Mess'.

Two months after the spectacular events over Copenhagen, the sad news arrived that 616 Squadron, the RAF's first jet squadron, was not to survive the post-war rundown,

Officers' mess invitation, Lubeck.

No.616 Squadron pilots at the end of hostilities at Lubeck. *Standing, left to right:* Woodacre, Stoddart, sqn clerk, unknown, Winder (Eng), Howell (Adj), Epps, Moon, Hobson, Gosling, Miller, Mason (MO), Watts. *Middle row:* Ridley, Clegg, Wilson, Rodger, Barry ('B' Flt Cdr), Wg Cdr Schrader (CO), Gaze ('A' Flt Cdr), George, Ellis (Eng), Mullenders. *Front row:* Amor, Easy, Kistruk, Cooper, Dean, Jennings, Packer, Wilkes.

and on 31 August the squadron was re-numbered 263 Squadron, and left France shortly afterwards, headed for RAF Acklington, in Northumberland. However, although the very disappointed air and ground crews were not to know, this was by no means the end of 616 Squadron's association with the Meteor.

No.616 (South Yorkshire) Auxiliary Air Force Squadron had the unique distinction of being the RAF's first jet squadron when it re-equipped with the Meteor F.1 aircraft in July 1944. It was the only Allied squadron to operate jets during the Second World War. Whilst the pilots rejoiced with the rest of the free world at the cessation of hostilities, celebrations were tinged with slight regret that they had not been able to use the jet to greater effect. The aircraft had been rushed into service, at a time when much further development was still necessary, not least on the engines and the cannons. The pilots had a very short time to convert from the single-engine, tail-wheel Spitfire before going back into combat in the twin-engine jets. It proved itself effective against the V-1 threat, but other commitments prevented it being fully utilised in this arena. In its ground attack role, in the hectic final phase of the war, it was not making use of its speed and high ceiling. The real test that 616 had been waiting for never came, and although the aircraft's successes were relatively few, by the end of the war the Meteor was well established in RAF service.

CHAPTER EIGHT

POST-WAR YEARS

It was not long before the famous Auxiliary Air Force squadrons were reintroduced, and twenty were reformed on 5 June 1946, including 616 Squadron.

With the auxiliaries re-forming in their own local areas, it was to RAF Finningley, in the heart of South Yorkshire, that 616 returned. Not unnaturally, former squadron members were eager to join the new 616, and it was expected that the squadron would be reunited with its Meteors in the fighter role, so it was something of a surprise to discover that 616 had been designated as a night-fighter squadron, to be equipped with the Mosquito NF 30, and two Airspeed Oxford trainers for instrument flying and twin-engine conversion training for new pilots.

Appointed to command the squadron was Selby-born Squadron Leader Ken Holden DFC, one of the founder members who had served with 616 throughout the Battle of Britain. On 8 November 1946, his adjutant wrote to all the airmen who had been the originals:

Squadron reunion dinner at the Danum Hotel, Doncaster, 24 May 1946. *Left to right:* Ken Holden, Alderman E.H. Shaw (Mayor), Duke of Portland (Hon Air Cdre), Denys Gillam.

Mosquito NF XXX at Finningley.

> The Commanding Officer has directed me to write to you as an old Squadron member, to
> ascertain if you are at all desirous of rejoining. It is hoped to have as many old members back
> as possible and consequently their application will be considered favourably.

Many took up the offer, including Harry Mason and Arthur Radcliffe, who had been
among the very first entries of 1938, and it was not long before the first of the auxiliaries
started to arrive. The aircrew included a number of wartime veterans, including Group
Captain Denys Gillam, DSO and two bars, DFC and bar, AFC, and 'Buck' Casson DFC;
both having flown with the squadron during the Battle of Britain. Another former
squadron pilot who joined was Jim McCairns DFC and two bars, MM, who had been shot
down in 1941, but escaped later from a POW camp. Also joining was Dennis Barry, Croix
de Guerre, who had been one of the first squadron pilots to convert from the Spitfire to
the Meteor in 1944. Other pilots with distinguished wartime records arrived, but all came
with far lower ranks than they had held during the war. This also applied to the ground
crew, where ex-officers were happy to opt for duties as SNCOs, just to be part of 'their'
squadron again.

The first regular officer to be appointed was Flight Lieutenant W.P. Swaby, who was
to be the assistant adjutant for duties with the training flight. A few days later, Flight
Lieutenant R.M. Pugh AFC arrived to be the adjutant. The first of the navigators, the first
to serve on the squadron, Flight Lieutenant C.F. Plimmer DFM, arrived to fill the post
of squadron navigation officer. The first task for this regular cadre was to obtain suitable
accommodation, and the squadron was allocated a complete barrack block and one of the
five main hangars.

No.616 Squadron aircrew at the summer camp, RAF Tangmere, 1948. *Left to right:* Harland, Pugh, Gillam, Ayton, Sqn Eng Off, unknown navigator, Barry, Lister, Casson, Holden (CO), Westwood, Terrington, Ingoldby, Kneath, Golitely.

Formation of 616 Squadron Mosquitoes.

The peacetime auxiliary squadrons had a small cadre of regular officers and airmen, but the great majority were part-time members, who attended lectures and ground training one night a week, with flying at the weekends. Each squadron deployed to a regular RAF airfield for a two-week summer camp of concentrated training.

The early post-war years saw a slow build up in squadron strength, with some notable landmarks. In recognition of the outstanding service of the auxiliary squadrons, on 16 December 1947, HM King George VI gave permission for the 'Royal' prefix. 13 June

Squadron Leader Ken Holden and squadron ground crew admire the Freedom of Doncaster, Silver Salver, December 1948.

1948, was a very sad day for 616. Flying Officer 'Mac' McCairns was air testing a Mosquito (NT 423) when an engine failed. He set the aircraft up for a forced landing, but the aircraft crashed half a mile from the airfield boundary, and he and AC2 E. Shaw, who was flying as a passenger, were killed.

The squadron's first summer camp, held at Tangmere from 8-21 August, was a great success, with high-level intercepts and cine-gun and air-to-ground firing forming the main exercises of the concentrated training period. Shortly after returning to Finningley, there came the popular announcement that the squadron would revert to a day-fighter squadron, with the promise that 616 would, once again, be equipped with jets. With this in mind, all new pilots would be trained initially on the Harvard, and the squadron received the first of these, KF 720, on 27 May 1948. The year was brought to a fitting climax when the squadron paraded in Doncaster to receive the Freedom of Entry into the County Borough of Doncaster 'on all ceremonial occasions with all customary privileges'. The Mayor, Alderman P. Judd, in the presence of the squadron's honorary air commodore, His Grace The Duke of Portland, handed the Scroll of Freedom, with an inscribed silver salver, to Squadron Leader Ken Holden.

616 Squadron started its re-birth as a jet squadron on 21 January 1949, when Meteor F.3 (EE 307) flew into Finningley. Throughout the spring there was a steady flow of Meteors to replace the Mosquitoes, and six pilots had converted to the jet fighter by the end of February. The final operational detachment with the Mosquito took place in March, with firing details on the Skipsea Range, and the last Mosquito (NT 283) departed for 15 MU on 6 May, with the final Meteor F.3 arriving a few days later. On 12 June the last of the former Mosquito pilots, Pilot II A.A. Smith, converted to the Meteor, and the squadron

flew to RAF Thorney Island for the summer camp as an all-jet squadron again. The arrival of the Meteor T 7 (VZ 463), and the departure of the last of the Oxfords, completed the re-equipment programme. Dennis Barry had been one of the first of the wartime Meteor pilots with 616, and, after rejoining the squadron in 1948, he had been flying the Mosquito. He recalls:

> I had enjoyed the Mossie very much, particularly since it was so capable on one engine, unlike the early Meteors we had flown at the end of the war. However, I was very pleased when we received our new Meteors and I found that I settled back into the routine very quickly.

The first two pilots to convert to the Meteor T.7 were Bob Jones, who had been awarded the DSO in Bomber Command, and Sheffield schoolmaster Ken Bown, who had flown Spitfires in the Middle East. Ken recalls how much faster the Meteor appeared, and that much emphasis was placed on practising asymmetric flying.

On 1 November the squadron was transferred from Reserve Command to 12 Group in Fighter Command, losing the squadron coding of RAW on its aircraft, reverting to the wartime code letters of YQ. With this change it became RAF policy to 'affiliate' the auxiliary squadrons with a regular squadron, and 616 established an excellent association with 263 Squadron, based at RAF Horsham-St-Faith, near Norwich. This was particularly appropriate, as 616 had become 263 Squadron at the end of the war when the auxiliaries had been disbanded, and all had to 'hand their number plates' to a regular squadron. This system of associating a regular and an auxiliary squadron to work together as a Wing proved highly successful, and 616 made many visits and combined exercises with 263, the first coming on 11 February 1950, when practise interceptions were carried out under the control of the Neatishead Air Defence Radar Unit.

The squadron recruiting campaign about to depart from outside one of Finningley's hangars.

The squadron suffered its first loss of a Meteor (EE 472) on 8 January. Dennis Barry explained:

I was the leader of a formation of three and, after take off, we carried out a snake climb, entering cloud at 1,500 feet, and we climbed through solid cloud until we broke out on top at 25,000 feet. After completing our interception exercise we commenced the descent. After entering the cloud I encountered severe icing and both engines flamed out. Thus I also lost the pumps providing the auxiliary services including the cockpit de-icing. With the Pennines close by and not being absolutely sure of my position, I was in a bit of a dilemma (!). I got a good vector to the airfield and got into the overhead but still in cloud at

Pilots return from a sortie at Horsham-St-Faith during the sector exercise of March 1950. *Left to right:* Barry Kneath, Denys Gillam, 'Buck' Casson, Bob Jones.

Summer camp at Tangmere, August 1950. The new code YQ has been applied to the aircraft.

Farewell dinner to Squadron Leader Ken Holden DFC, at Finningley, December 1950. The Earl of Scarborough, Squadron Leader 'Buck' Casson and Finningley's station commander, and Group Captain C. O'Grady enjoy a drink.

1,500 feet. With no ejector seats fitted to the early Meteors, I felt I had little alternative but to jump, although I was very conscious that others who had tried had been killed when they hit the tail. However, as I was below 1,000 feet I had no choice and slowed the aircraft to stalling speed then put on some bank as I jumped. This carried me away from the tail and I had a good descent. Unfortunately the ground was frozen solid and I broke my leg on landing.

In many respects this was a remarkable escape, and one of the very few successful unassisted escapes from a jet fighter.

The 1950 summer camp was held at Tangmere, with most of the operational pilots achieving twenty hours flying, concentrating on air-to-air and air-to-ground firing exercises, with the pilots under training flying the Harvard and Meteor T 7. The end of the year was tinged with sadness when two of the great names of 616 Squadron retired. The commanding officer, Ken Holden, who had been the very first auxiliary pilot to join the squadron in 1938, and had recently been awarded the OBE, handed over command to his friend and fellow pre-war auxiliary, 'Buck' Casson, from Sheffield. Also retiring was one of the RAF's greatest pilots, Denys Gillam, who had been the most successful 616 pilot during the Battle of Britain, and who had ended the war as one of the most highly decorated RAF pilots, with three DSOs, two DFCs and an AFC. Ken Bown summed up everyone's feelings: 'Denys was a great leader who acted as a father figure to the younger pilots. I flew as his number two, and learnt a great deal from him. It was easy to understand why he was nicknamed 'Killam' Gillam. He was absolutely fearless.'

Despite his unique record and outstanding courage, he was a quiet, modest Yorkshireman from Malton, and he died in July 1991, just two days after attending the squadron's annual reunion held at the Battle of Britain Memorial Flight, at RAF Coningsby.

1951 was to be the busiest year in the post-war history of the squadron. On 16 April, the CO announced that all the auxiliary squadrons had been called up for three months, as the Korean War crisis developed. The part-timers reported to Finningley, and a number of the ground crew received VIP treatment on arrival. Engine fitter Aircraftman 2 Joe Stenton picked up six others in his large black Buick car. The highest ranker in the car was a corporal, but, on approaching the main gate, the armed sentry leapt to attention and gave an immaculate salute. As Eric Browne commented, 'how fleeting is fame?' In the event, it was very fleeting, since the senior service policeman (SP) witnessed the incident and soon restored the correct hierarchy by detailing the seven airmen to extra duties.

The whole squadron deployed to RAF Acklington, on the Northumberland coast, for an Armament Practise Camp (APC), with a concentrated training phase of air-to-air firing. Almost 100 effective sorties were flown in a two-week period, with the CO leading the way with forty per cent of his shots hitting the flag. During this period, the Meteor F.4 started to replace the old F.3s, and ten of the latter flew out to Flight Refuelling at Tarrant Rushton on 18 May. The squadron was detached to RAF Church Fenton to spend a month working alongside the regular fighter squadrons and, by the end of this period, 616 had reached peak efficiency, and was ready to assume a full operational role in Fighter Command. However, within a month, the call-up period was terminated and the squadron reverted to the familiar weekend routine.

One of the immediate problems facing all auxiliary squadrons, following the end of the call-up period, was to try and retain the high level of proficiency that had been achieved. This was, of course, virtually impossible, as personnel found it increasingly difficult to be away from their full-time weekday jobs. However, training continued at weekends, with GCI controlled practise interceptions, under Patrington's control, an exercise pinnacle that culminated in the interception of four USAF B-45 bombers.

The Meteor F.4 era was short lived, and by the end of 1951 the squadron started to receive the definitive mark of the Meteor, the classic F.8. The Meteor F.8 reigned supreme in Fighter Command during the early 1950s, serving with over forty RAF squadrons. With its increased stability, afforded by the re-designed tail, the Derwent 8 engine, better cockpit canopy design and ejector seat, the Mark 8 was a great improvement on its predecessors, and much liked by the pilots.

The summer camp of 1952 saw the squadron deploy overseas for the first time, when ten F.8s and the two T.7s flew to RAF Celle, in West Germany, but, with no live-firing facilities, the squadron had to content itself with cine sorties. The annual major UK air defence exercise, Exercise Ardent, took the squadron to Church Fenton to form a Wing with 19 and 609 (West Riding) Squadrons. Convoy patrols and practise interceptions against the Lincolns and B-29 Washingtons of RAF Bomber Command provided realistic training.

In September it was announced that 616 Squadron had been awarded the coveted Esher Trophy, awarded to the most efficient of the twenty-one auxiliary squadrons. This was only the third occasion that the trophy had not been awarded to one of the London squadrons.

Pilots at the Armament Practise Camp at Acklington during the three-month call up for the Korean War, May 1951. *Standing, left to right:* Clark, Smith, Westwood, Witteridge, Blow, Humphries. *Seated:* Kerr, Harland, Kneath, Casson (CO), Jackson, Barry, Bown.

Pilots prepare to depart to Celle for the summer camp, August 1952. *Left to right:* Higginbotham, Hamilton, Kneath, Jones, Casson, Harland, Kerr, Smith, Furness.

At an impressive ceremony at RAF Doncaster, with the whole band of Headquarters Fighter Command in attendance, Major General the Earl of Scarborough KG, GCSI, GCIE, TD, presented the trophy to the squadron commander, Squadron Leader L.H. Casson DFC. In his speech, the Earl of Scarborough mentioned that this was the first time the trophy had come to Yorkshire in its twenty-six years of existence, and he hoped that it would remain there for a number of years.

A reception for officers and guests was held in the officers' mess at RAF Doncaster, and for SNCOs, airmen and guests in the Drill Hall. A glittering array of senior officers attended, including the squadron's former station commander of 1942, Air Chief Marshal Sir Basil Embry KBE, CB, DSO, DFC, AFC, the Commander-in-Chief, Fighter Command. Also present was Lady Riverdale and the Mayor and Mayoress of Doncaster.

Tragedy struck at the end of 1952, when two pilots were lost over the North Sea during a night practise interception exercise, under the control of Patrington GCI. Flight Lieutenants Barry Kneath DFC and John Harland, took off in WH 455 and WH 473, and climbed in formation. They acknowledged instructions from Patrington with a call that they had split, and were in visual contact at three miles. Nothing further was heard from either aircraft, and it was assumed that they had collided. Distress flares were seen twenty-three miles off Whitby, but an intensive sea and air search found no trace of the pilots or their aircraft.

The increasing shortage of pilots was partially offset in 1953, with the introduction of former national service pilots. Understandably, they were relatively inexperienced, and the training flight was kept busy. An extremely successful summer camp was conducted

Presentation of the Esher Trophy, 27 September 1952. *Left to right:* Jolly, Jones, Kneath, Pringle (Eng Off), Casson (CO), Hutchinson, Kerr, Higginbotham, Watt (MO).

at Takali, in Malta, with no less than 410 hours being flown. The Meteors transited via Biggin Hill and Istres, in Southern France, getting airborne with wing overload tanks and a ventral tank. The highly successful detachment was marred when Sergeant A.A. Smith was seen to dive vertically into the sea off Valetta Harbour in Meteor WE 862.

On returning from Malta, the squadron was soon travelling again, but this time it was only a few miles down the road to Wymeswold, to form a Wing with 504 (County of Nottingham) Squadron for Exercise Momentum. This provided a wide range of targets, with interceptions against Canberras at 40,000 feet, and Sea Furies of the Fleet Air Arm at wave-top level, as they attacked shipping off the East Coast. With 156 sorties flown, it was one of the most successful post-war exercises ever.

The unfortunate spate of accidents continued with the loss, on 27 September 1953, of Pilot Officer George Furness, in WE 912. He was seen to eject at 1,000 feet, near Spalding, but he died before his parachute had deployed fully. On 22 May 1954, the long-serving Flight Lieutenant Harry Blow DFC was lost in WH 278. He was leading a formation of four aircraft in a snake climb when he entered cloud at 1,500 feet in a starboard turn. His No.2, Flying Officer Willby, had increasing difficulty staying in formation and, as speed built up, broke away and flew on instruments alone, finding himself in a steep diving turn to port. He recovered and climbed above the cloud, but his leader dived into a field near Sandtoft and was killed instantly.

The annual summer camps, and the major autumn air defence exercises, remained key elements of the year for the auxiliary squadrons, and over the next two years 616 returned to Malta and visited Oldenburg in Germany.

The latter part of 1954 was notable for a number of reasons. The directors of Rolls-Royce presented the squadron with a silver rose bowl to commemorate the 10th Anniversary of 616 becoming the first RAF jet squadron. The squadron's former wing leader from

Ground crew refuel the Meteor F.8 (WH 474).

A Meteor F.8 fitted with long-range wing tanks, on the dispersal at Takali, Malta, during the summer camp of 1953.

Frank Wooton's painting of Dixie Dean's successful 'tip up' destruction of a V-1. The painting commemorated the 10th Anniversary of the Gloster Meteor entering service with No.616 Squadron. Mr P.G. Crabbe, the managing director of Glosters, presents the painting to Squadron Leader 'Buck' Casson (CO) and Flight Lieutenant Dennis Barry (Flt Cdr). October 1954.

Tangmere, Group Captain Douglas Bader, visited Sheffield to open the squadron town headquarters at Hallam Lodge. He renewed his friendship with the CO, 'Buck' Casson, who had flown with him throughout his time at Tangmere. They had both been shot down on the same sweep over Northern France, on 9 August 1941. Following the opening, when the house was floodlit, a reception was held and, in addition to the many service guests, the Lord Mayor and Lady Mayoress of Sheffield, the Mayor and Mayoress of Doncaster and

Master and Mistress Cutler also attended. Finally, on 1 November, 'Buck' Casson handed over command of the squadron to a regular officer, Squadron Leader W.G. Abel.

'Buck' Casson was a great loss to the squadron, having served for almost ten years – the last four as squadron commander. For his outstanding services he was awarded the Air Force Cross, to add to his DFC, and was awarded a second clasp to his Air Efficiency Award.

During 1955, the squadron moved from its spiritual home at Finningley to Worksop, to allow the former to be re-developed as a V-bomber station. The squadron continued to exercise from Horsham-St-Faith whenever possible, but the squadron record book makes frequent mention of the increasing difficulties experienced by the Meteors in reaching high flying targets, and the superior performance of the new breed of fighters and bombers. The venerable Meteor was showing its age.

In the New Year's honours list the name of Flight Lieutenant Ken Bown appeared. He had served in the squadron longer than any other pilot, and during his time had accumulated just over 1,000 hours in the Meteor. He had been the flight commander for three years, and for his services he was awarded the AFC – the last auxiliary to receive this award.

Following the ill-fated Suez crisis, there was increasing speculation regarding the future of the auxiliary squadrons. On 10 January 1957, all the squadron commanders were called to a conference at the Air Ministry, where the Chief of Air Staff, ACM Sir Dermot Boyle, announced that the squadrons were to disband within two months, and all flying was to cease immediately. The announcement came as a severe blow, and immediate press and

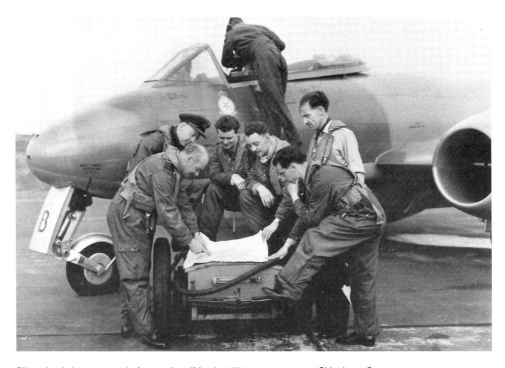

Pilots check the route map before setting off for the 1954 summer camp at Oldenburg, Germany.

Opening by Group Captain Douglas Bader of the squadron's town HQ at Hallam Lodge, Sheffield, on 30 October 1954. Bader poses with AVM G. Ambler (West Riding T&AFA), Squadron Leader Jack Dodd (OC 2616 Squadron) and his old friend Squadron Leader 'Buck' Casson DFC, AFC (OC 616 Squadron).

A formation of Meteor F.8s with the squadron markings prominent, November 1952.

Squadron Leader 'Buck' Casson hands over command of No.616 Squadron to Squadron Leader W.G. Abel RAF.

television campaigns were launched to save the squadrons, but to no avail. There was to be no reprieve.

It fell to the squadron commander, Bill Abel, to break the news to the men of 616 Squadron. He recalls the difficult task:

> I think we knew that the writing was on the wall. With the advent of the all-weather fighter there was less need for the gun-equipped day fighters. It was, of course, terribly sad, but the men took it marvellously well. But that was no surprise to me. They were a wonderful crowd and I couldn't keep them away from the Squadron. How their families and employers put up with it all I will never know. During the Suez crisis the Squadron was inundated with phone calls asking when we would be called forward. That was the spirit of the Auxiliaries; it was a privilege to command such marvellous men.

During February, most of the Meteors were flown away to a maintenance unit for scrapping. On a grey and sombre day, 3 March 1957, No.616 (South Yorkshire) Squadron, Royal Auxiliary Air Force Squadron, paraded for the final time, at RAF Worksop, under the command of their last CO, Squadron Leader Bill Abel. His Grace the Duke of Portland KG inspected the parade and took the salute at the final march past. At the conclusion of his address, the honorary air commodore returned the Freedom Scroll to the Mayor of Doncaster, Mrs E.R. Dougal-Callender JP, who, in a short but graceful response, promised it a permanent home in the Mansion House. The Duke used the occasion to make a rare boast on behalf of 616: 'Our record is a proud one. We won eleven DFCs, one DFM, two

On the disbandment parade of the squadron, its honorary air commodore, the Duke of Portland, hands the Freedom of Doncaster scroll to the safe keeping of the Mayor of Doncaster, Mrs E.R. Dougal-Callender JP.

AFCs and two Croix de Guerres. Our tally of enemy planes destroyed was magnificent. This day is bitter sweet for us all.'

Perhaps the flight commander, Ken Bown, who had served for nine years on 616, best summed up the feelings of all who served in the auxiliaries, when he said:'It was the other half of your life; nothing could replace the squadron or the comradeship.'

So, one of the greatest and most loyal of RAF formations, the flying squadrons of the Royal Auxiliary Air Force, passed into history with a record of service that was equalled by their sister squadrons of the regular RAF, but was never surpassed.

Today, the men of 616 Squadron meet annually in South Yorkshire to recall the comradeship and the spirit that binds them together. Their modesty prevents them from thinking that they are different from their many thousands of RAF colleagues, but history relates that the men of 616 (South Yorkshire) Squadron had the unique distinction of being the RAF's 'First Jet Squadron'.

EPILOGUE

In the summer of 1987, two of the squadron's post-war ground crew, Eric King and Ben Schofield, both of Doncaster, decided to try and contact old comrades with a view to a reunion. The response was greater than they had anticipated, so they decided to preceed much encouraged.

In August, they approached the recently appointed station commander at RAF Finningley (the author) to broach the subject. They were as yet unaware that they had struck lucky, since the new man was a South Yorkshireman who had a long-held and deep interest in 616 Squadron and its unique history. Agreement to hold a reunion at Finningley was a formality.

One of the station's navigation instructors, Flight Lieutenant Ken Delve, himself a keen RAF historian, was given the task of liaison officer. On 6 November 1987, fifty veterans arrived at Finningley, and spent the day as the guests of the station, with a full programme of visits arranged for them, culminating in a session in the officers' mess bar with the young aircrew students, where many stories of the halcyon days of the squadron were told.

This immensely successful reunion led to the establishment of a tradition. Over the following months, a surplus RAF Meteor F.8 was acquired and painted in the full squadron colours, including the markings of one of the former COs, Squadron Leader 'Buck' Casson DFC, AFC. At the 1988 reunion, during a poignant ceremony at the main gate, in the presence of the Mayor of Doncaster, Councillor Ron Gillies, the Meteor was dedicated by the station padre, and unveiled by the squadron's last CO, Squadron Leader (later Group Captain) W.G. Abel.

The third reunion, on 16 June 1989, was also a special occasion. To celebrate the 25th Anniversary of its Chequer Road Museum, the Doncaster Council welcomed members and their wives to view an exhibition of memorabilia, and attend a lunch at the Museum. The author had the privilege of opening the exhibition and meeting the Mayor of Doncaster and the Mayors or Chairmen of Bassetlaw, Retford and Rotherham, who also attended. The day was rounded off with a dinner in the officers' mess at Finningley.

The annual reunion continued at Finningley until the airfield was closed in 1995. In 1994, the Association held an additional reunion at RAF Manston, to celebrate the 50th Anniversary of the Meteor entering RAF service with 616. The Martin Baker Company allowed their Meteor test aircraft to join the party before a dinner was held in the officers'

The Meteor F.8 guardian is lowered into place at the main gate of RAF Finningley, May 1988.

Group Captain W.G. Abel, 616 Squadron's last CO, unveils the plaque for the Meteor gate guard at Finningley, 10 June 1988. In attendance are Eric King (Squadron Association Secretary), Group Captain G.R. Pitchfork MBE (station commander, Finningley) and Mr Ronald Gillies (Mayor of Doncaster).

No.616 Squadron's Battle of Britain veterans, Denys Gillam, 'Cocky' Dundas and 'Buck' Casson at the Squadron Association's annual reunion at Coningsby, 28 June 1991. In the background are Max Williams and Arthur Radcliffe, who served as squadron ground crew during the Battle.

The first Meteor pilots, posing in front of the Martin Baker Meteor, reunited at the squadron's annual reunion at RAF Manston, 29 July 1994. *Left to right:* Sam Easy, Ned Kelly (Aus), Eddie Epps, Freddie Packer, Jack Ritch (Can), Dennis Barry, Mike Cooper (Kenya), Geoff Amor, Sid Woodacre, Bob George.

'Buck' Casson unveils the squadron Meteor at the Yorkshire Air Museum assisted by the Museum Trustee Derek Reed.

mess. This was a particularly memorable occasion, since no less than ten of the original 616 Squadron Meteor pilots were in attendance, and the event carried on until the early hours of the morning, and, as can be imagined, all those early flights were recounted.

Subsequent reunions were held at various locations including RAF Cottesmore and with the Battle of Britain Memorial Flight at RAF Coningsby. With the closure of RAF Finningley, negotiations were opened with the Ministry of Defence to acquire the Meteor. These were successful and the aircraft was transferred to the Yorkshire Air Museum on the former RAF bomber airfield at Elvington near York. On 3 May 1996, over thirty veterans attended a lunch as guests of the Museum and 'Buck' Casson unveiled the aircraft and handed over the aircraft's logbooks to the curator. The aircraft has remained on permanent display and a few years ago was refurbished and re-painted. Hence, a 616 Squadron presence in Yorkshire has been maintained.

15 February 2005 provided a particular highlight for some Association members when they were introduced to HM the Queen and Prince Philip at a reception held at the RAF Club to commemorate 80th Anniversary of the Royal Auxiliary Air Force. The Association President, Group Captain Bill Abel, and members Dennis Barry and Harry Mason, represented 616 Squadron and were introduced to the Royal party.

With the inevitable decline in Association membership, the annual reunions have become gentler. For the past ten years they have been centred on Doncaster where the Earl of Doncaster Hotel has become the Association's second home and where the squadron's silver and Freedom Scroll are displayed for the evening thanks to the great generosity of the Chief Executive of the Doncaster Metropolitan Borough Council and the Curator of the Doncaster Museum.

APPENDIX I

THE SQUADRON'S ESCAPERS AND EVADERS

During their training, all RAF aircrew were briefed that it was their *duty* to escape from captivity should they be shot down and fall into enemy hands. There were very many gallant attempts but of the 10,000 Royal Air Force prisoners in permanent camps in Germany, just twenty-nine reached safety. Such statistics give a measure of the immense difficulty of making a successful escape.

The chances of returning home safely were, of course, significantly higher if downed airman could avoid capture by successfully evading the enemy. As the war progressed in Western Europe, the organisations for assisting Allied airman to evade capture improved significantly, but the odds were still heavily against them. For every successful evader passed along the lines, ten were captured, and many brave agents were lost.

As the bomber offensive over German-occupied territory intensified, and losses increased, it was inevitable that the number of aircrew finding themselves unexpectedly in enemy territory would grow considerably. Not surprisingly, the flow of successful evaders also increased, and many individual bomber squadrons could no doubt claim a number of 'home runs'.

However, it is very doubtful if any squadron could claim such a high proportion of returning aircrew as 616 Squadron. Equipped throughout the war with single-seat fighters, no less than five pilots evaded capture, and two others made outstanding escapes from German POW camps. With the squadron spending long periods on home defence duties, this record becomes even more remarkable.

During the long hot summer of 1941, the squadron flew offensive sweeps, circuses and escort missions over Northern France. Casualties were high, but no less than four of the squadron pilots lost during this period were to evade capture and find their way back to Great Britain.

Sergeant D.B. Crabtree

First of the 616 Squadron evaders to arrive back was Sergeant Douglas 'Cuthbert' Crabtree, whose home was near Halifax in Yorkshire. He had enlisted in the RAF Volunteer Reserve

Douglas Crabtree with the
French family that sheltered him.

as a pilot in July 1937, during a period of rapid RAF expansion. After completing his flying training, he was posted to Filton where he joined 501 (County of Gloucester) Squadron, equipped with Hurricanes. In May 1940, 501 flew to North France to reinforce the fighter squadrons supporting the Advanced Air Striking Force, and Crabtree was lucky to escape with minor injuries when the Bombay transport aircraft he was travelling in crashed near Betheniville, with the loss of a number of lives.

Crabtree fought throughout the Battles of France and Britain, before joining 616 Squadron from 57 OTU, on 12 May 1941 – a time when the pace of operations by the Bader Wing, over France, was gathering momentum, with sweeps almost daily. Losses mounted and, on 3 July, Douglas Crabtree failed to return from an offensive patrol.

At 10.40, eleven squadron aircraft had taken off from Westhampnett on an offensive patrol in support of bombers attacking Lille. Shortly after crossing the French coast, the squadron was engaged by Me 109s. Crabtree became detached from the group, but, seeing another lone Spitfire being attacked by enemy fighters, dived to give assistance, claiming one aircraft before cannon shells smashed into his aircraft's engine. Hoping to glide to the coast, he came under renewed attack and was forced to bale out of his burning Spitfire IIA (P 7980) at 3,000 feet, landing in a cornfield near Hazebrouck. His aircraft had just thirty-two hours flying time.

Having buried his parachute, Crabtree hid in a hedge until dusk, and then set off towards the coast, but within a short time he walked straight into a five-man German patrol. On landing, he had hurt his ankle, and made out that he could hardly walk. He was well treated, taken to a farm and locked in a barn for the night. Thinking he could not walk, the patrol left with the intention of returning for him in the morning. Seizing his chance, Crabtree made a hole in the wall and escaped, setting off to walk through the night. Over the next few days he stayed with various French farmers, who gave him clothes and food, before he was directed to a house in Lillers, where he met up with French Canadian Sergeant Larry Robillard.

On 24 July, they travelled by train to Bethune, where they joined Pilot Officer Duval, another French Canadian pilot, and three British soldiers. The whole party travelled on

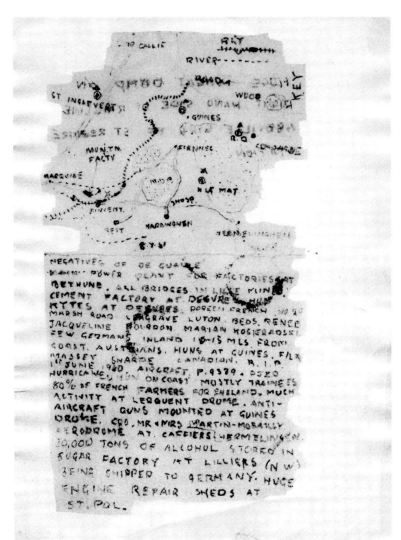

The notes Crabtree made on cigarette papers that he was able to hand over at his debriefing in London by MI9 officers.

to Paris via Abbeville, and the following day took the train to Tours, and then on to St Martin Le Beau, a small village twenty kilometres to the east. Here they set off on foot to cross the Line of Demarcation, just to the south. After resting in a farmhouse during the day, they set off to walk the twenty kilometres to Loches, where they caught the train to Chateauroux and then on to Marseille, which they reached on 28 July. Three days later they travelled to Perpignan, before setting off to walk across the frontier. After crossing the mountains, they caught a train to Barcelona where they were sheltered in the British Consulate. By mid-August they had been transferred to Gibraltar. Crabtree was able to get a lift on a Sunderland flying boat, and arrived at RAF Mountbatten near Plymouth on 26 August.

Crabtree brought back some valuable information regarding German defences and the attitudes of the French people. He made notes on a cigarette paper, which he secreted into the lining of his cap. Had he been captured and the information found, it is unlikely that he would have survived. In the event he was able to pass on this valuable information during his debriefing by officers of MI9.

Shortly after re-visiting 616 and narrating his experiences to his colleagues, Derek Crabtree was awarded a Mention in Despatches for his resolve and fortitude in successfully escaping and evading capture. He did not return immediately to operational flying, instead becoming a flying instructor, initially with 54 OTU at Church Fenton, before training as a night fighter pilot. A year after his return to England he was commissioned to fly Beaufighters in the North African campaign. He retired as a flight lieutenant in 1946. Sadly, he was killed in a civil flying accident in June 1950.

Squadron Leader E.P.P. Gibbs

Squadron Leader Patrick Gibbs joined 616 as a flight commander in June 1941. He was a regular officer with eight years service, having served previously on 232 and 66 Squadrons. He had been a pre-war fighter pilot, but spent the first eighteen months of the war as a flying instructor on squadrons outside the combat area. With no operational experience, he was keen to see action, so he volunteered to return to fighters. During his time as an instructor he had become an expert aerobatic pilot, and this skill was to pay handsome dividends within a few weeks of joining the squadron.

As predicted by his colleagues, Gibbs did not last long in combat. He took off at 13.10 on 9 July 1941, led by Wing Commander Douglas Bader, to escort Stirlings on a bombing raid to Mazingarbe in Northern France. Twenty miles inland the Me 109s arrived, and numerous combats broke out, with Gibbs and his number two taking on two of the enemy fighters. In a head-on attack he despatched one and, as he turned to attack the second, a cannon shell smashed into his engine, which soon stopped as glycol poured out. He started to glide down to make a wheels-up landing when two enemy fighters closed in on him. Realising that he was a sitting duck, he jettisoned his canopy, rolled the aircraft on its back and continued to glide to the ground, hoping to give the impression that he was dead. A few feet above the ground, he rolled back the right way up and executed a perfect crash landing in a stubble field. Setting fire to his Spitfire II (P 8070), he was racing for the hedgerows before the German pilots could turn back.

Gibbs had come down twelve miles east of Le Touquet. Following the cardinal rule of getting as far away from the crash site as quickly as possible, he immediately set off at a brisk walk, using the hedgerows as cover, until he came across a farm worker and his wife, who directed him to a farmhouse where he received great hospitality. After resting overnight, he walked through the day and into the night, headed for another farm where he was treated 'magnificently'. He rested for five days, which allowed the injuries he sustained in the crash landing to heal.

At this stage of the war escape lines had not been established, but Gibbs' helpers proved to be extremely resourceful and brave. A doctor smuggled him across the boundary of the 'Zone Interdit', near Amiens, on the pretext that he was suffering from an acute appendicitis. The doctor's niece then escorted him on the train to Paris, where a medical student and his wife gave him shelter. Forged identity cards and civilian clothes were provided, and fourteen days after being shot down, a young female medical student arrived to escort him to her aunt's house in Perpignan.

Squadron Leader E.P.P. Gibbs at Westhampnett a few days before he was shot down.

They travelled on the night train to Salies de Bearn, thirty miles east of Biarritz, where they crossed the Demarcation Line into unoccupied France. To avoid the more stringent identity card checks, they travelled on to Perpignan using the slow local trains. Once in Perpignan, he said goodbye to his brave companion and, after a few hours sleep, he was briefed by a Frenchman on how to cross the border into Spain. He took the local train to Banyuls, close to the border, and left the station unhindered. As he was leaving the town, a gendarme, who recognised his identity card as a forgery, accosted him. Despite declaring his true identity, and pleading to the gendarme's patriotism, he was taken into custody.

The next day he was taken to an internment prison called St Hippolyte du Fort, near the town of Nimes. Here he met four other British officers, and some ninety soldiers, who had tried to escape the advancing German Army a year earlier, but had failed. The camp was run on civilised terms, with the officers allowed out on parole to the local town, on the understanding that they would not escape. In addition to affording some pleasant social opportunities, parole allowed them to study the local area, make important contacts, and meet the heads of escape organisations. Gibbs was also able to send a telegram to his wife reporting that he was 'safe and well in Unoccupied France'. After six weeks, this was the first indication to the squadron that he had survived, and the RAF was able to remove him from the missing in action list.

After three weeks, Gibbs withdrew his parole agreement on the basis that it was an unfair advantage over the guards! He had made a simple plan to escape. Just as darkness fell on the evening of 18 August, he approached the main gate with a colleague who had arranged for the gate to be opened on the pretext that he was going out on parole. He then created a diversion, which allowed Gibbs to dash through the gate and down the street to a pre-positioned bicycle, where he cycled away. Once well clear, he discarded the bicycle and set off to walk the seventeen miles to Nimes, through the night, to a house arranged by the escape organisation. The next day a member of the organisation took him by train to Marseille.

In Marseille he met up with a party of four other British evaders. They were taken individually to Perpignan, where a Spanish guide met them and drove them into the Pyrenees. Stopping short of the border, they left the road and set off to walk forty miles over the mountains, climbing to 10,000 feet. At 21.00, on 26 August, they crossed the border and descended to a farm owned by relations of the guide. After resting for the night, they walked to the nearest railway station and took the local train to Barcelona where they contacted the British Consul who arranged for them to be taken to Madrid.

Here, the consul arranged for their repatriation, and two weeks later Gibbs arrived in Gibraltar.

On 16 September, Patrick Gibbs boarded a Sunderland flying boat, arriving at Plymouth the next day. He had been away just over three months, and arrived back three weeks after Douglas Crabtree's return. He had followed all the evaders' rules. He had attended lectures, carried his own survival kit and extra money, left the scene of his crash immediately, and headed straight for the unoccupied zone. His escape was well prepared and simple. He was fortunate to meet many brave helpers, but his own approach was commendable.

Shortly after his return, he and another evader were invited to have lunch with the Prime Minister, who wished to hear of their experiences. During the discussion that followed, Winston Churchill asked Gibbs if he had obtained the name of the French gendarme who had arrested him near the Spanish border. On learning that he had not been identified, Churchill retorted in a jocular vein, 'Pity, we could have put him on the list to be dealt with when we have won the war.' A few weeks later, Patrick Gibbs was awarded a Mention in Despatches.

Sergeant L.M. McKee

In December 1941, 616 Squadron's third successful evader arrived back in England via Spain. The Devonian, Sergeant Lawrence McKee, was one of numerous losses suffered by the squadron during the hectic summer of 1941. The squadron had lost Bader and 'Buck' Casson just five days before McKee baled out of his stricken Spitfire VB (W 3514), at lunchtime on 14 August.

The Tangmere Wing had taken off at 14.00, under the leadership of Wing Commander Woodhouse AFC, leading his first offensive sweep as the new wing leader. It was a relatively quiet sortie by recent standards, and the Wing saw little of the enemy. But, on return, Sergeant McKee was missing. He had been posted to 616 from 66 Squadron just five weeks earlier, on the day that Patrick Gibbs had been shot down.

McKee had baled out ten miles south-east of Calais, near the village of Norkerque. Landing some distance from his crashed aircraft, he hid in a ditch until it was dark, before risking calling at a farm. Fortunately, the Germans had already searched the area, and the farmer put him up for the night. He set off the next morning dressed in an old suit and a pair of farmer's boots. He soon met another Frenchman who obtained two bicycles and rode with him to Calais. He was sheltered in various farms and houses in the Calais and Boulogne areas over the next three weeks.

On 6 September, McKee met up with Flight Lieutenant A. Winskill of 41 Squadron, also of the Tangmere Wing. In fact, Winskill had been shot down minutes before McKee had baled out, and had landed outside the same village, where the local people had also sheltered him. They formed a party, together with three British soldiers, and found themselves being moved by the same organisation that had moved Douglas Crabtree just six weeks earlier. With forged identity papers, McKee's party followed the same route through Abbeville to Paris, and on to Tours. Here they changed to the branch line and, after crossing the River Cher, were escorted on foot across the Line of Demarcation, north of Loches, on 24 September. After walking into the town of Loches, they were moved quickly by train to Marseille.

From Marseille they moved straight to Perpignan, where they remained for ten days whilst a guide was found to take them across the border into Spain. After travelling by train to Aix Les Thermes, via Toulouse, they met their guide, who escorted them into Spain through Andorra. Once in the Province of Barcelona, they were taken to the British Consul. After a few weeks of negotiation with the Spanish authorities, McKee arrived in Gibraltar, and was flown to England in a Sunderland, arriving at Plymouth on 18 December.

As with so many successful evaders, McKee owes his freedom to evading the enemy in the first few crucial hours, along with the good fortune of making early contact with patriotic Frenchman, who passed him into the escape lines with the minimum delay. Others were not so fortunate.

Sergeant J.A. McCairns

With three evaders home from France, via Gibraltar, it was the first of 616 Squadron's escapers who was next to return. Sergeant Jimmy 'Mac' McCairns had joined the squadron at Kirton in Lindsey during the squadron's build up, after the heavy losses incurred during the Battle of Britain. He soon established a reputation as a fearless pilot who constantly sought out the action. The summer of 1941 was a hectic one for the Tangmere Wing, and he flew on many offensive escorts and sweeps either in the sections led by Johnnie Johnson or by 'Cocky' Dundas. On 30 June his aircraft was hit during a low-level attack, but he managed to bring his damaged Spitfire back to Westhampnett. Seven days later, he was not so lucky.

At 13.30 on 6 July, McCairns took off in his Spitfire IIA (P 8500) from Westhampnett, for a wing patrol over St Omer led by Wing Commander Bader. McCairns' aircraft had been delivered from 39 MU to the squadron just two days earlier. About fifteen miles inland, Me 109s engaged his section, and his brand new aircraft was badly damaged by cannon fire. Diving to ground level, he set off to return across the Channel, but was hit in the radiator by light flak and shortly afterwards his engine seized. He crash landed in a field 300 yards from the beach at Gravelines. He had been hit in the leg by shell splinters and, with the canopy jammed closed, two Luftwaffe personnel soon captured him and carried him to the flak position 100 yards away.

His wounds were dressed before he was transferred to a military hospital in St Omer, where his leg was operated on successfully. Five days later he was taken by road to Dulag Luft, in Frankfurt, where he met up with his flight commander, Colin MacFie, who had been shot down four weeks earlier. After two days of processing, he was included in a party of fifty-three NCOs, and taken by train to Stalag IXC, in Bad Sulza. The train was lightly guarded, but his injured leg and the loss of his boots prevented an escape attempt.

From the moment he was captured, McCairns devoted all his efforts to gaining his freedom. By making meticulous plans, creating escape aids, and having his mind focussed on little else, he increased significantly his chances of success. Such dedication brought its reward within ten months.

Within hours of arriving at Stalag IXC he started to gain the moral ascendancy over his guards. Required to give a thumbprint for his camp identity card, he smeared his thumb with chewing gum to give a false impression. He spent the next four months making various escape aids. He started to hoard food, and he exchanged some of his clothing with a

French inmate who had some tent cloth, from which he made a corset arrangement to go under his outer clothing. He also made maps and a compass, and obtained pliers from a Serb prisoner who worked in a local factory. Finally, he made a groundsheet, which he designed to wrap round his right leg and fit under his trousers.

By late November 1941 he was ready to make his first escape attempt. He teamed up with another RAF sergeant, and their initial plan was to cut a way through the wire fences to the outer camp, where they would hide up for the day before scaling the single outer fence. Unexpectedly, an opportunity occurred to leave for the outer camp with a Belgian working party. With all their escape aids immediately available, they were able to seize the opportunity. Leaving in the early morning, before it was light, they moved to the outer camp with the Belgians, braking away before they reached the work place. Still

Sgt J.A. McCairns.

in darkness, they were able to scale the 9 foot outer fence with the aid of specially made reinforced mittens.

Getting clear of the camp quickly, they made for the nearby Thuringian mountains, and hid up for the day. As it got dark, they headed for the local railway line, with the aim of getting near Weimar. There was an airfield near the town, from which they planned to steal an aircraft. Soon a slow goods train passed, and they jumped into an empty wagon. Within six hours they were in Weimar, where they left the goods yard and started to walk out of the town. As they stopped to work out the direction of the airfield, a man in a uniform surprised them and, not believing their story, started to march them towards the town. As they entered the residential area the two British airmen broke away, running in opposite directions. McCairns got clean away, but unfortunately his colleague ran into an army patrol.

Once clear, he set off to find the railway line, as it left the town. He followed a single line until it joined a main line siding, where he found an empty coach and slept for a few hours. He spent the whole of the next day hiding in the lavatory of the coach. After dark he left the siding for the main line, where he was able to jump into a goods wagon. The train travelled through Erfurt and, soon after leaving Gotha, he dozed off. At 07.00, on 22 November, a flashlight was shone in his face. He raced away, but found the train was stationary in the well-lit centre of Warburg station. There was no escape, and he was soon re-captured.

After a preliminary interrogation, he was taken to Oflag VI B, near Warburg, where he spent four days in solitary confinement. He was then taken back to Stalag IXC by train. En route he spent most of his time making observations for his next attempt. On his return, most of his equipment was discovered, and he spent a further six days in solitary.

Over Christmas and New Year he devoted considerable thought to escaping again. His first attempt had provided him with a great deal of experience and ideas, and he carefully analysed every aspect. Deciding that the guards would not expect an escape attempt in winter, he decided to take advantage and leave as soon as possible. He concluded that a winter escape could only be successful if he travelled by train, and thus civilian clothes would be essential. He then met up with a Belgian officer who had also been recently returned from an unsuccessful escape attempt, and they agreed to make their next escape together. He spent the following few days altering his uniform to look like civilian clothes.

On the night of 21 January the two took their clothes into the Belgian barracks where a tailor made last minute alterations, and a Frenchman briefed them on escape routes, which they had to memorise. After resting for a few hours, they walked out at 06.00 with the first Belgian working party. Following a similar route to his first attempt, McCairns and his Belgian colleague soon scaled the fence and, discarding their uniform outer clothes, to be picked up by the Belgian prisoners, they set off for the local town. They walked quickly, and went straight through Bad Sulza to Apolda, some eight miles further on. They reached the town in less than two hours, and within an hour they had caught a train to Kassel, arriving at 14.30.

McCairns lost sight of his companion in Kassel but, as arranged, took a train to Koblenz, which he reached nine hours later. Leaving the station, he spent the night in a coach in a siding, before returning to the station, where he caught sight of his fellow escaper. They bought tickets to Mainz, and caught a train within a few hours. Approaching Mainz he became confused and left the train one stop too early. Once clear of the station, he quickly gained his bearings, and walked into the town to the main station, where he bought his next ticket. He travelled on to Garolstein and St Vith. Before his escape he had been briefed to avoid St Vith, renowned for its strict scrutiny of identity cards. With this in mind, he jumped from the train as it approached the station.

As he left the train there was a heavy snowstorm, which made travel difficult, and he was forced to walk on the sleepers of the rail track. Eventually he found a small shed and rested for the night. In the morning he travelled along the road to Weismes, where he caught a train to Malmedy, a journey which took fifteen minutes. He left the station at noon and walked straight into a blizzard. He realised that he could not attempt to cross the Belgian border in daylight, so he dug a snow hollow behind a hedge and waited for darkness.

As darkness fell, he set off to walk west and, after wading across a river and walking through foot-deep snow, unknowingly crossed the German–Belgian border in the early hours. He soon came to a main road, which he followed until he arrived at a church. He struck a match and saw that the notices were written in French. He approached a nearby house, and spent the rest of the night in the garden shed. For company he had a pig and a few chickens. At 07.00 he approached a Belgian in the yard, who took him into the house where his father was listening to the BBC morning news in French.

Before escaping, his Belgian colleague had briefed him to make for a hotel in Francorchamps. After breakfast, and once his clothes were dry, he set off, and arrived in the small town a few hours later. The hotel proprietor was upset and would do nothing except put McCairns in touch with a local official, who proved to be very hospitable. After a meal and a sleep lasting eighteen hours, he was escorted through Spa, reaching Brussels six days after his escape. He was now in safe hands, and he was taken care of by the brave Belgian and French members of the 'Comet' Line – arguably the most effective of all the escape lines.

After eight weeks resting in safe houses in Brussels, he was taken to Paris on 25 March. Travelling to Bayonne by train, he was taken over the Pyrenees and on to Madrid by guides, arriving in Gibraltar a month after leaving Brussels. On 30 April 1942, he was flown to Hendon airfield, the fourth RAF man to return after escaping from a German POW camp. Shortly afterwards it was announced that he had been awarded the Military Medal for his courage.

It would be invidious to identify one of the twenty-nine successful escapes by RAF personnel as being more meritorious than others. However, the escape by 'Mac' McCairns must be recognised as a classic and a model for all would-be escapers. From the moment he was captured he made escape his top priority, spending a great deal of time gathering information and making mental notes. He was observing routines at railway stations, identifying uniforms and assessing ways of escape. Once in captivity, he started to gather intelligence, prepare escape kits and clothing, and study the detailed layout of the camp to identify weak spots. Of particular importance, he made a plan, which he kept simple. After recapture, following his first attempt, he analysed his performance and noted all the lessons he had learned. Those features that had worked, he used again on his second attempt to great advantage.

On both attempts he recognised the need to get as far away from the camp as quickly as possible. It is remarkable how few difficult moments he had to counter during his successful escape – a testimony to his precise planning and his constant vigilance. All escapers need some luck, but McCairns needed less than most because he had, in abundance, the greatest attributes needed for a successful escape. He had the right frame of mind, was determined, resourceful and, above all, courageous.

It came as no surprise to his colleagues that McCairns declined the opportunity to take up a non-operational appointment that was routinely offered to escapers. He elected to return to operational flying. It was typical of the man that he should choose one of the most dangerous and demanding roles. After a 'refresher' flying course, he joined the Lysander Flight of 161 Squadron, better known as the Moonlight Squadron. By joining such a unit, he felt that he was repaying those gallant resistance workers who had played such a major part in his return to England. He was to become one of the most successful of all the 'pick up' pilots, flying thirty-two operational sorties to deliver agents and to pick up returning agents, evaders, French dignitaries and officials. For his gallant work with 161 he was three times awarded the Distinguished Flying Cross, and the French government invested him with the Croix de Guerre.

After the war he returned to civilian life in South Yorkshire, but immediately rejoined 616 Squadron, which had returned to its native county. On 13 June 1948, he took off in a Mosquito NF30 (NT 423) with a member of the squadron ground crew, AC2 Shaw. During the flight the port engine failed as a result of a glycol leak and, as he was approaching RAF Finningley for an emergency landing, the aircraft crashed half a mile short, killing both occupants. So ended the life of a very gallant pilot who had contributed so much to the proud record of 616 Squadron.

Sergeant P.T. Wareing

Sergeant Philip Wareing had the rare distinction of being the only RAF fighter pilot to be shot down over enemy territory during the Battle of Britain. Two and half years later he was to achieve the more worthy distinction of arriving in England after an outstanding escape from captivity deep in Poland.

Wareing had joined the peacetime RAF Volunteer Reserve in 1938 and, after completing his training, was one of a number of NCO pilots who joined 616 Squadron to bring it up to a full operational complement.

On 22 August, Wareing scrambled from RAF Kenley with Green Section, and Me 109s soon engaged them. Seeing Green 3 in trouble, he dived on the tail of its aggressor and, after a brief fight, shot the Me 109 down in flames. Three days later the squadron had already been airborne twice when twelve aircraft were scrambled at 18.20, this time to intercept a raid heading for Maidstone at 15,000 feet. Three of the enemy aircraft were destroyed, but two of 616's NCO pilots failed to return. One was Philip Wareing.

As the squadron engaged the bomber force of twenty Dornier 17s, mid-Channel, the escorting Me 109s dived to attack and broke up the squadron formation. Wareing engaged one of the fighters and scored hits, forcing the enemy aircraft to turn for France. In the heat of the battle, Wareing gave chase to the damaged aircraft but, before he could destroy it, other fighters attacked him. He shot one down, but was soon hit and his Spitfire I (R 6966) was so badly damaged in the engine and radiator that he was forced to bale out a mile south of Calais, close to a German fighter airfield.

He was observed descending in his parachute and, as an enemy motorbike and sidecar arrived to take him prisoner, he had time to wipe the recognition signals of the day from one of his hands. He was taken to the nearby Luftwaffe base where he was treated as a comrade and offered cognac. His membership of the German Alpine Club before the war added to the camaraderie, and he was well entertained. Before leaving the base, he gave his name to a German pilot who was himself shot down over England a few days later. At his subsequent interrogation, he was able to tell the intelligence officer of his meeting with Wareing, providing the first indication of his survival to his British comrades.

After travelling to Brussels, he was flown to the transit POW camp at Dulag Luft, near Frankfurt. Following the initial interrogation, he was transferred to Stalag Luft I, in Barth, situated on the Baltic coast. He was to remain there until April 1942, when he was transferred to Stalag Luft III, in Sagan, where he was involved in a number of tunnel schemes. During his time at Sagan he heard from fellow prisoners that escape was easier from Poland, so he took the opportunity to volunteer to go with a party of officers, as their orderly, to Oflag XXI B, in Schubin, some 150 miles west of Warsaw, arriving towards the end of September.

He soon set about preparing an escape kit. He altered his RAF uniform, and obtained other items of clothing. Food was stockpiled, and he got hold of a compass and maps. Shortly after his arrival at Schubin, he learnt that RAF sergeants who had a good reputation were allowed to go out on working parties. On 16 December 1942, he was able to join a bread party to the nearby railway station. As the lorry backed up to the railway truck, a fellow prisoner dropped some bread on the line by accident. Wareing immediately jumped down between the lorry and the wagon, got underneath the truck and crossed the railway tracks, escaping into the fields without being seen. It was just getting dark.

He made for the woods beyond the village of Blumenthal, and then turned to the north-east. Throughout the night he made steady progress, resting occasionally. Initially, he intended to rest by day, but he pressed on once it was light in order to get well away from

Philip Wareing photographed shortly after his return to England, following his escape to Sweden. In this photo he has recently been commissioned.

the camp. By mid-afternoon he had reached the town of Blomberg, some twenty miles north of Schubin. Here he was able to take an old bicycle, and he set off along the Danzig road, heading for Graudenz, where he hoped to board a ship for Sweden. The bicycle was in poor condition, so he walked and cycled alternately. The road was well signposted and, with a full moon, he made good progress.

Having turned off the Danzig road to cross the river Vistula, he came to a well-guarded bridge. The guards were questioning two Germans, so he slipped past and continued his journey to Graudenz, which he reached at 08.00 the following morning. He was disappointed to find no Swedish ships in the docks, and thus decided to head for Danzig. At the railway station he exchanged his bicycle for a new one, which had just been left by a German. He immediately moved out of the town and had to re-cross the bridge over the Vistula, which he again negotiated successfully, taking advantage of an argument between the guards.

He cycled into the country and helped himself to some milk from a churn beside the road. Arriving at Mewe in the late afternoon, he slept in a haystack for eight hours. Riding his bicycle, he arrived in Danzig two days later and immediately set out to find the docks. Initially he was unable to locate a Swedish ship, but in the early morning of 20 December he found a ship, which was loading coal. He hid amongst woodpiles to observe movements, and then, avoiding the police patrols, walked up the gangplank as soon as the guard had turned away. He made his way directly to the forward hold, where he remained for the rest of the day.

Late in the day, when the hold was three-quarters full, some Russian prisoners arrived to trim the cargo. Wareing was able to alert them and they did not give his position away. As soon as they departed he buried himself in the coal. Next morning the Germans searched the boat for two hours, but he was not discovered, and shortly after 09.00 on the morning of 21 December the boat sailed. He remained in hiding for three days when hunger and thirst forced him to go on deck where a member of the crew saw him. Some of the crew looked after him for the remainder of the voyage and, as they docked in Halmstead, the captain was alerted. He was handed over to the police and, on 28 December, a member of the British Legation accompanied him to Stockholm. After a few days of rest he was flown to Leuchars, on 5 January 1943.

Philip Wareing had made a textbook escape. He had made good preparations and was able to react quickly once an opportunity arose. He was well equipped, and he had a simple plan. When a chance occurred, he took it immediately and, once free, he got away from the area of his camp as quickly as possible. Without taking undue risks, he was bold, and his two crossings of the river Vistula, his entry to Danzig docks, and his direct boarding of the

Swedish ship are testimony to his cool and courageous approach to escape. In recognition of his skill, determination and courage, he was awarded the Distinguished Conduct Medal, a very rare award to a member of the RAF.

On his return, he was in demand as a lecturer, and he toured various airfields to recount his story and to offer advice to aircrew that might find themselves in a similar situation. He spent the remainder of the war as a flying instructor, and retired as a flight lieutenant in 1946. He worked in air traffic control for some time before joining the motor industry. He died in 1987.

Squadron Leader P.W. Lefevre DFC

Next of the 616 Squadron evaders to return was the squadron commander. Squadron Leader Peter 'Pip' Lefevre had been in command of 616 for just twelve days when he was shot down over the Brest Peninsula at 11.30, on 16 April 1943.

Having joined the RAF from Cambridge University in early 1938, 'Pip' Lefevre had already had an exciting and adventurous time on flying operations before taking command of the South Yorkshire squadron. Posted to 46 Squadron, he flew his first wartime patrol two days after war was declared, and was in air combat a few weeks later, sharing in the destruction of a He115. He fought in the ill-fated Norway campaign and, returning in a motor vessel, avoided the tragic loss of so many of his squadron colleagues when the aircraft carrier, *Glorious*, was sunk. Fighting in the Battle of Britain, he claimed two destroyed and one probable, before leaving for Malta in *Ark Royal*. Flying off the carrier to Malta, at the maximum range of his Hurricane, he was soon involved in some of the fiercest fighting of the Battle for Malta. He claimed further kills, was promoted to squadron leader and

Squadron Leader Philip Lefevre DFC, the squadron CO for a few days before he was shot down.

given command of 126 Squadron, equipped with Hurricanes. He was awarded the DFC in December 1941, shortly before he returned home for an instructional tour.

Returning to operations, 'Pip' Lefevre took command of 616 in April 1943. Flying a Spitfire VI (BS 114), he led his first sweep on the 16th, when the squadron took off from Perranporth, at 12.30, to act as close escort to twenty-four Liberators bombing Brest. The formation encountered intense heavy flak at 22,000 feet over the target, and Lefevre's aircraft was hit. Unable to regain control, he baled out at 12,000 feet and landed in a field just south of Ploughin.

Whilst descending under his parachute, Lefevre noticed many people cycling and running beneath him, and on landing he found himself surrounded by some seventy French civilians and one gendarme. With some knowledge of French, he realised that offers of help were being made, and gratefully accepted a drink. He discarded his parachute and life jacket, which promptly disappeared into the crowd. Unfortunately, his box of escape aids was in his life jacket and he was unable to retrieve it. Whilst cutting the tops off his flying boots, he was warned that the Germans were approaching, so he headed for a hedge where he lay down. Two young boys arrived and advised him to hide right in the bushes, which he did until sunset.

After dark a farmer arrived with food and drink, and the following morning returned with civilian clothes. The Germans conducted an intensive search, and Lefevre remained in hiding for a further two days. Hearing that the Germans had taken seven local people as hostages, he decided to move on with the help of the farmer's friend. Dressed in a civilian suit, he was rowed across the Aber-Benoit estuary to a house in the village of Plouguerneau, where he came under the control of the 'Comet' line. The line had suffered some serious reverses in the recent past, and he was transferred to the 'Burgundy' line and taken to Paris where he joined up with twelve other evaders. Within a few days, the group travelled to Etables to rendezvous with a submarine, but sea and moonlight conditions were unsuitable, and the risky operation was called off.

Returning to Paris, the group waited for escorts before travelling by train to Pau, and then on to the foothills of the Pyrenees. Using a smugglers trail, they climbed into the mountains and over the Spanish border. Soon after crossing into Spain they were arrested and imprisoned in Pamplona jail. The British Ambassador secured their release within two weeks. Peter Lefevre arrived in Gibraltar on 13 July, just three months after he was shot down. The next day he boarded a Dakota and was flown to Whitchurch near Bristol.

'Pip' Lefevre returned to 616 in August to relate his experiences and to fly a Spitfire again. Three days later he was posted to command 266 (Rhodesia) Squadron, flying Typhoons from Exeter. During December and January he accounted for an Me 109 and shared in the destruction of a Fw190 and Ju88, bringing his total to five destroyed, with a further five shared destroyed, a probable and a damaged. On 6 February 1944, he took off from Harrowbeer, at the head of his squadron, to attack shipping in the Abervrach estuary near Brest. Flying at 1,000 feet, he was hit by flak and was seen to bale out over the estuary. But this very gallant pilot was lost.

Flying Officer M.H.F. Cooper

Last of the 616 Squadron evaders was Flying Officer Mike Cooper, who had travelled from Kenya to join the RAF in early 1941. He had joined the squadron at Kings Cliffe in

Mike Cooper, with his wife Kitty, travelled to France as soon as the war was over to meet the families who had sheltered him. Here they are pictured with the Coudrez family, who looked after him shortly after he was shot down.

April 1942, and by October he had come down twice in the English Channel and been rescued.

After many sweeps and escorts over Northern France during the first half of 1943, Mike Cooper took off from Ibsley on 16 August 1943, leading Blue Section in his Spitfire VI (BR 987), as escort to twelve Venturas bombing Tricqueville airfield. As the bombers left the target thirty miles south-east of Le Havre, Cooper's aircraft developed engine trouble and he was forced to bale out at 12,000 feet. He landed in a tree and, once he had freed himself, set off for nearby woodland, where he met a fifteen-year-old boy who introduced him to two men. These two men provided him with overalls, and he set to work in the fields. There was much German activity as they searched for him, so he decided to leave the area. After walking for three days, he arrived at the town of Bellou, where he met a man who offered him shelter. Three families sheltered him for two months, and all befriended him. During this time, the Resistance, who organised his onward journey, contacted him. He met up with two of the crewmembers of a Canadian Halifax, and they were transported to the coast where they were to board a submarine. During three hazardous weeks, when several helpers were arrested, the idea was abandoned and they were moved from house to house, before being taken to Paris, where they were hidden for ten days.

They were then taken by train to the town of Ruffec, one of the main collecting centres for the escape 'lines', where they came under the care of Marie (Comtesse de Milleville or Mary Lindell) – organiser of the 'Marie-Clare' line. Here they met up with Flight Lieutenant A. Mc Sweyn RAAF, and Captain R. Palm SAAF, both having made daring escapes from German POW camps. With the arrival of a Greek officer, the party was large enough for an escorted crossing of the Pyrenees. The first attempt, via Foix, failed, and the party returned to Ruffec. After five days another attempt through Pau, Claron and Tardet was made. With two guides they set off on a journey which they estimated would take twelve hours.

They had been told that the journey would be easy, so they took no food or drink. They set off at midnight in the pouring rain. One of the party suffered a heart problem, and they had to rest until morning. The sick man had to be helped, and this slowed the party considerably. By mid-afternoon the rain had turned to snow, and then a full blizzard, making the going even more difficult as the snow deepened. In the intense cold, one of the guides died, and the whole party suffered from hypothermia and frostbite. After thirty-six hours they stumbled into a hut and were able to light a fire and dry out. Setting off the next morning, the remaining guide became lost, and McSweyn took charge of the exhausted party. They walked to the nearest town and gave themselves up to the Spanish police. The British Consul soon arranged for their release, and on 20 December 1943 they arrived in Gibraltar via Madrid. The next day, Mike Cooper was flown back to Whitchurch airfield, near Bristol.

After recovering from his ordeal, Mike Cooper rejoined 616 Squadron, who were then stationed at Exeter. Shortly afterwards, in June 1944, he was amongst the first group of the squadron's pilots to convert to the Meteor jet fighter. Involved in attacks against the V-1 rockets and, later on ground strafing sorties, as the squadron moved through Holland and Germany, he remained with 616 until VE Day, by which time the squadron had reached Lubeck.

Summary

Understandably, the circumstances of the two escapes, and the five evasions made by the men of 616 Squadron, are different. And yet there are common themes. Perhaps the most important was to have the right frame of mind; an overpowering desire not to be captured or to escape from captivity. All recognised the need to get clear of the immediate area of their POW camp or aircraft crash site as soon as possible. They also appreciated the need for quick decisions and a plan, and those who escaped were prepared in advance and able to seize a chance opportunity to make for freedom. Certainly, presence of mind, decisiveness and a certain ability to act or bluff were important. Undoubtedly luck was a feature, particularly when approaching strangers for help. No doubt many brave men just knocked on the wrong door. Although possessing these other qualities reduced the importance of luck, every successful escaper and evader would readily acknowledge that luck had played a part. Without doubt, the most important characteristic was courage, and plenty of it was needed. The seven men of 616 Squadron possessed it in abundance.

APPENDIX II

ROLL OF HONOUR

21.02.40	Flight Lieutenant A.N. Wilson
04.06.40	Pilot Officer E.W.S. Scott
04.08.40	Sergeant J.P. Walsh
07.08.40	Pilot Officer R.A.D. Smith
25.08.40	Sergeant T.E. Westmoreland
26.08.40	Flying Officer G.E. Moberly
26.08.40	Sergeant M. Ridley
30.08.40	Pilot Officer J.S. Bell
27.09.40	Flying Officer D.S. Smith
08.11.40	Pilot Officer F.S. Roberts
10.03.41	Sergeant B. Bingley
21.04.41	Sergeant R.L. Sellars
24.04.41	Sergeant T.F. McDevette
21.06.41	Pilot Officer E.P.S. Brown
25.06.41	Sergeant J.A.H. Jenks
25.06.41	Sergeant R.C. Brewer (RNZAF)
21.07.41	Sergeant S.W.R. Mabbett
21.07.41	Sergeant F.A. Nelson
06.08.41	Sergeant B.W. Hopton
22.09.41	Pilot Officer E.H. Burton
22.09.41	Sergeant J.B. Slack
27.09.41	Pilot Officer R.G. Sutherland (RCAF)
06.01.42	Flight Sergeant M.M. Waite (RCAF)
12.04.42	Pilot Officer H.R. Strouts (RCAF)
12.04.42	Pilot Officer M. Lepel-Cointet (Free French)
13.04.42	Sergeant G.L. Davidson (RNZAF)

26.05.42	Pilot Officer L.B. Ware (RNZAF)
03.06.42	Pilot Officer P.J. Moore
20.06.42	Sergeant W.A. Clouston (RNZAF)
30.07.42	Sergeant D. Lee
11.08.42	Sergeant R.H.J. Noad
19.08.42	Sergeant N.W.J. Coldrey
01.11.42	Sergeant P.S. Smith (RNZAF)
18.02.43	Flying Officer P.J. Blanchard
05.04.43	Flight Lieutenant P.B. Wright DFC
16.04.43	Flight Lieutenant G.B. MacLachlan
15.06.43	Pilot Officer R.J. Sim (RNZAF)
31.08.43	Flight Sergeant R. McKillop
31.08.43	Sergeant P.W. Shale
21.10.43	Pilot Officer A.F. Smith
21.10.43	Sergeant E.R. Cole
05.11.43	Sergeant W. Gordon
03.12.43	Flight Sergeant F.W. Rutherford
01.04.44	Flight Sergeant D.E. Johnston (RAAF)
22.05.44	Pilot Officer G.E. Prouting
12.06.44	Flight Lieutenant G.A. Harrison
19.06.44	Warrant Officer R.A. Hart (RAAF)
15.08.44	Warrant Officer D.A. Gregg
25.08.44	Corporal W.M. Harding
29.04.45	Squadron Leader L.W. Watts DFC
29.04.45	Warrant Officer B. Cartmel
13.06.48	Flying Officer J.A. McCairns DFC★★, MM
13.06.48	Aircraftman 2 E. Shaw
11.12.52	Flight Lieutenant B. Kneath DFC
11.12.52	Flight Lieutenant J.W. Harland
03.07.53	Sergeant A.A. Smith
27.09.53	Pilot Officer G. Furness
22.05.54	Flight Lieutenant H. Blow DFC

APPENDIX III

HONOURS AND AWARDS

Officer of the Order of the British Empire

7 June 1951   Squadron Leader K. Holden DFC

Bar to Distinguished Flying Cross

26 June 1942   Acting Flight Lieutenant J.E. Johnson DFC
19 January 1943   Acting Flight Lieutenant F.A.O. Gaze DFC

Distinguished Flying Cross

12 November 1940   Flight Lieutenant D.E. Gillam AFC
15 July 1941   Acting Squadron Leader K. Holden
5 August 1941   Acting Flight Lieutenant H.S.L. Dundas
8 August 1941   Acting Flight Lieutenant C.H. Macfie
16 September 1941   Flight Lieutenant L.H. Casson
19 September 1941   Acting Squadron Leader H.F. Burton
30 September 1941   Pilot Officer P.W.E. Heppell
30 September 1941   Flying Officer J.E. Johnson
4 November 1941   Pilot Officer A. Smith
26 June 1942   Pilot Officer R.D. Bowen RCAF
3 November 1942   Pilot Officer R.G. Large
15 December 1942   Squadron Leader H.L.I. Brown
23 July 1943   Acting Flight Lieutenant L.W. Watts

George Medal

6 January 1942   Aircraftman 1st Class K. Bland
6 January 1942   Leading Aircraftman (Temp Sergeant) G.G. Williams

Distinguished Flying Medal

30 September 1941 Sergeant J.C. West RNZAF

Air Force Cross

1 June 1953   Squadron Leader L.H. Casson DFC
1 January 1957 Flight Lieutenant K. Bown

Distinguished Conduct Medal

14 December 1943 Sergeant P.T. Wareing

Military Medal

18 August 1942 Flight Sergeant J.A. McCairns

British Empire Medal

14 June 1945   Flight Sergeant W. Young

Croix de Guerre

27 May 1944   Pilot Officer J. Clerc (Free French)
25 July 1945   Squadron Leader D.A. Barry

MID

11 June 1942   Sergeant D.B. Crabtree
11 June 1942   Squadron Leader E.P.P. Gibbs
1 January 1945 Flying Officer M.H.F. Cooper
14 June 1945   Flying Officer T.D. Dean
14 June 1945   Flying Officer J.K. Rodger
14 June 1945   Flying Officer I.T. Wilson

APPENDIX IV

COMMANDING OFFICERS

November 1938	Squadron Leader the Earl of Lincoln
September 1939	Squadron Leader W. K. Beisiegel
May 1940	Squadron Leader M. Robinson
September 1940	Squadron Leader H.F. Burton DFC
September 1941	Squadron Leader C.F. Gray DFC & Bar
February 1942	Squadron Leader H.L.I. Brown DFC
January 1943	Squadron Leader G.S.K. Haywood
April 1943	Squadron Leader P.W. Lefevre DFC
April 1943	Squadron Leader P.B. Lucas DFC
July 1943	Squadron Leader L.W. Watts DFC
July 1944	Wing Commander A. McDowall DFM & Bar
May 1945	Wing Commander E.E. Schrader DFC
August 1945	Disbanded
July 1946	Squadron Leader K. Holden DFC
December 1950	Squadron Leader L.H. Casson DFC
November 1954	Squadron Leader W.G. Abel
March 1957	Disbanded

APPENDIX V

SQUADRON BASES

01.11.38	Doncaster	18.03.44	West Malling
23.10.39	Leconfield (Dets at Catfoss & to Rochford)	24.04.44	Fairwood Common
		16.05.44	Culmhead
19.08.40	Kenley	21.07.44	Manston
03.09.40	Coltishall	17.01.45	Colerne (Det at B.58 Melsbroek)
09.09.40	Kirton-in-Lindsay		
26.02.41	Tangmere	28.02.45	Andrew's Field (Det at B.58 Melsbroek)
09.05.41	Westhampnett		
06.10.41	Kirton-in-Lindsay	01.04.45	B-77 Gilze Rijen
30.01.42	Kings Cliffe	13.04.45	B-91 Nijmegan
03.07.42	West Malling	20.04.45	B-109 Quakenbruck
08.07.42	Kenley	26.04.45	B-152 Fassberg
29.07.42	Great Sampford (Dets to Hawkinge & Ipswich)	03.05.45	B-156 Luneberg
		07.05.45	B-158 Lubeck
23.09.42	Tangmere	31.08.45	Disbanded
29.10.42	Westhampnett	10.05.46	Finningley
02.01.43	Ibsley (Det to Harrowbeer)	23.05.55	Worksop
17.09.43	Exeter (Det to Fairwood Common)	10.03.57	Disbanded

APPENDIX VI

616 SQUADRON AIRCRAFT AND AIRCREW LOSSES

Date	Name	Age	Casualty	Aircraft	Serial	Action	Location
1940							
21.02.40	Flt Lt A.N. Wilson	33	Missing	Spitfire I	K 9810	Descend into sea	Nr Hornsea
01.06.40	Plt Off J.S. Bell		Safe	Spitfire I	K 9948	Combat. Ditched	English Channel
04.06.40	Plt Off E.W.S. Scott	20	Killed	Spitfire I	N 3130	Crashed poor wx	2 NNW Rochford A/F
04.08.40	Sgt J.P. Walsh	20	Killed	Spitfire I	N 3271	Spun in	Kirton-in-Lindsay
07.08.40	Plt Off R.A.D. Smith	25	Killed	Spitfire I	R 6696	Night Fly	Nr Leconfield
22.08.40	Plt Off H.S.L. Dundas		Wounded	Spitfire I	R 6926	Combat. Bale out	Nr Dover
25.08.40	Sgt T.E. Westmoreland		Missing	Spitfire I	K 9819	Combat Me 109	Nr Maidstone
25.08.40	Sgt P.T. Wareing		POW	Spitfire I	R 6966	Combat	Nr Calais
26.08.40	Fg Off G.E. Moberley	25	KIA	Spitfire I	N 3275	Combat Me 109	Eastchurch
26.08 40	Sgt M. Ridley	24	KIA	Spitfire I	R 6701	Combat Me 109	Dungeness
26.08.40	Plt Off W.L.B. Walker	27	Wounded	Spitfire I	R 6633	Combat. Bale out	Channel off Ramsgate
26.08.40	Sgt P. Copeland		Wounded	Spitfire I	K 9827	Combat. Force land	Wye, Kent
26.08.40	Plt Off R. Marples		Wounded	Spitfire I	R 6758	Combat. Force land	Adisham, Kent
26.08.40	Plt Off E.F. St Aubyn		Wounded	Spitfire I	R 7018	Combat. Force land	Eastchurch
30.08.40	Fg Off J.S. Bell	23	KIA	Spitfire I	X 4248	Combat. Crashed	West Malling
01.09.40	Plt Off L.H. Casson		Safe	Spitfire I	R 6778	Combat. Force land	Kenley
02.09.40	Flt Lt D.E. Gillam		Safe	Spitfire I	X 4181	Combat. Bale out	Tonbridge
27.09.40	Fg Off D.S. Smith	26	DOW	Spitfire I	X 4328	Combat Me 109	Faversham
05.11 40	Flt Lt C.A.T. Jones		Wounded	Spitfire I	X 4055	Combat He 111	Spurn Head
08.11.40	Plt Off F.S. Roberts	23	Killed	Spitfire I	X 4056	Crashed	8 SE Kirton-in-Lindsay

1941

Date	Name	Age	Status	Type	Serial	Cause	Location
10.03.41	Sgt B. Bingley	24	Killed	Spitfire II	P 7662	Crashed	Steyning nr Worthing
21.04.41	Sgt R.L. Sellars	23	Missing	Spitfire II	P 7812	Patrol. Bale out	30 S Catherines Point
24.04.41	Sgt T.F. McDevette		KIA	Spitfire II	P 7736	Crashed. Flak	Maupertas A/F
05.05.41	Fg Off L.H. Casson		Safe	Spitfire II	P 7753	Combat. Bale out	Nr Littlehampton
21.06.41	Plt Off E.P.S. Brown		KIA	Spitfire II	P 7730	Circus. Shot down	NW Boulogne
23.06.41	Sgt D.W. Beedham		Safe	Spitfire II	P 7435	Bale out	English Channel.
25.06.41	Sgt J.A.H. Jenks	25	KIA	Spitfire II	P 8272	Circus. Shot down	Le Touquet
25.06.41	Sgt R.L. Brewer (NZ)	29	KIA	Spitfire II	P 7327	Circus. Shot down	Le Touquet
26.06.41	Sgt R.A. Morton		Safe	Spitfire II	P 7815	Sweep. Crash land	Bacton, Norfolk
03.07.41	Sgt D.B. Crabtree		Evaded	Spitfire II	P 7980	Circus. Shot down	Hazebrouk
05.07.41	Flt Lt C.H. MacFie		POW	Spitfire II	P 8651	Sweep. Bale out	Lille
06.07.41	Sgt J. McCairns		POW	Spitfire II	P 8500	Circus. Crash land	Nr Gravelines
07.07.41	Sgt R.D. Bowen		Safe	Spitfire II	P 8438	Circus. Crash land	Hawkinge
09.07.41	Sqn Ldr E.P.P. Gibbs		Evaded	Spitfire II	P 8070	Circus. Shot down	12 E Le Touquet
09.07.41	Sgt R.A. Morton		POW	Spitfire II	P 8386	Circus. Shot down	Nr St Omer
21.07.41	Sgt S.W.R. Mabbett	21	KIA	Spitfire II	P 8690	Circus. Shot down	Lille
21.07.41	Sgt F.A. Nelson	26	Killed	Spitfire II	P 8434	Crashed	Nr Worthing
06.08.41	Sgt B.W. Hopton	21	Died of Inj	Magister	L 5985	Crashed	Perranporth
09.08.41	Wg Cdr D.R.S. Bader		POW	Spitfire Vb	W 3185	Circus. Shot down	Nr St Omer
09.08.41	Flt Lt L.H. Casson		POW	Spitfire Vb	W 3458	Circus. Shot down	Nr Marquise
14.08.41	Sgt L.M. McKee		Evaded	Spitfire Vb	W 3514	Sweep. Bale out	10 SE Calais
21.09.41	Sgt J.C. Carter		POW	Spitfire Vb	AB 795	Sweep. Bale out	10 S, Le Touquet
22.09.41	Plt Off E.H. Burton	21	Missing	Spitfire Vb	W 3433	Sweep. Mid-air	1 S, Brighton
22.09.41	Sgt J.B. Slack	29	Killed	Spitfire Vb	W 3517	Sweep. Mid-air	1 S, Brighton
27.09.41	Sgt J.C. West (NZ)		Safe	Spitfire Vb	W 3655	Sweep. Bale out	Eng. Channel.
27.09.41	PO R.G. Sutherland(RCAF)	22	KIA	Spitfire Vb	W 3334	Sweep. Flak	5 SW, Abbeville
08.11.41	Wg Cdr D.R. Scott AFC	33	KIA	Spitfire II	P 8701	Circus. Shot down	Pas de Calais

1942

Date	Name	Age	Outcome	Serial	Aircraft	Event	Location
06.01.42	F.Sgt M.M. Waite (RCAF)	26	Killed	AA 923	Spitfire Vb	Convoy Patrol	20 E. Skegness
15.03.42	Sgt N.G. Welch		Injured	BL 345	Spitfire Vb	Landing	Wittering
27.03.42	Sgt C.J. Baxter (RAAF)		Safe	AD 459	Spitfire Vb	Mid-Air. Bale out	Hertfordshire
12.04.42	Plt Off H.R. Strouts (RCAF)		KIA	AD 375	Spitfire Vb	Sweep. Shot down	Hazebrouk
12.04.42	Plt Off M. Lepel-Cointet (FF)		KIA	AD 456	Spitfire Vb	Sweep. Shot down	Hazebrouk
13.40.42	Sgt G.L. Davidson (RNZAF)	26	Killed	AD 543	Spitfire Vb	Crashed	Wansford, nr Wittering
15.04.42	Sgt P.C. Miller (RAAF)		Injured	BL 754	Spitfire Vb	Circus. Ditched	4 S, Dungeness
25.05.42	Plt Off C.B. Brown		Wounded	BP 250	Spitfire VI	Combat. Do217	Nr Leicester
26.05.42	Plt Off L.B. Ware (RNZAF)	26	Killed	BR 172	Spitfire VI	Crashed	Dunholm, Nr Lincoln
03.06.42	Plt Off P.J. Moore	22	KIA	BR 191	Spitfire VI	Circus. Shot down	Le Touquet
20.06.42	Sgt W.A. Clouston (RNZAF)	21	Killed	AD 559	Spitfire Vb	Crashed	N Sheringham
30.07.42	Sgt M.H.F. Cooper (Kenya)		Safe	BR 167	Spitfire VI	Ramrod. Bale out	Off Dungeness
30.07.42	Plt Off R.G. Large		Safe	BS 108	Spitfire VI	Ramrod. Bale out	Eng Channel.
30.07.42	Sgt D. Lee	21	Killed	BR 243	Spitfire VI	Ramrod. Crash	App Biggin Hill
30.07.42	Plt Off J.R. Mace		POW	BR 597	Spitfire VI	Ramrod. Shot down	Nr Boulogne
11.08.42	Sgt R.H.J. Noad	19	Killed	BR 164	Spitfire VI	Crashed	Tollesbury, Essex
19.08.42	Sgt N.W.J. Coldrey (Rhod)	26	KIA	AB 529	Spitfire VI	Combat. FW 190	Dieppe
19.08.42	Flt Lt J.S. Fifield		Safe		Spitfire VI	Combat. Bale out	Eng Channel.
02.10.42	F.Sgt M.F.H. Cooper		Safe	BR 159	Spitfire VI	Circus. Bale out	Off Calais
01.11.42	Sgt P.S. Smith (RNZAF)	22	Killed	BR 186	Spitfire VI	Convoy Patrol	off Isle of Wight

1943

Date	Name	Age	Outcome	Serial	Aircraft	Event	Location
18.02.43	Fg Off P.J. Blanchard	21	Killed	BR 310	Spitfire VI	Crashed	10 S, Bournemouth
05.04.43	Flt Lt P.B. Wright DFC	22	KIA	BS 465	Spitfire VI	Ramrod. Shot down	10 N, Brest
16.04.43	Flt Lt G.B. MacLachlan	21	KIA	BS 245	Spitfire VI	Ramrod. Shot down	N of Brest
16.04.43	Sqn Ldr P.W. Le Fevre DFC		Evaded	BS 114	Spitfire VI	Ramrod. Flak	Brest
18.04.43	Sgt S.J. Fowler		Safe		Spitfire VI	ASR Sortie. Ditched	S of Swanage
15.06.43	Plt Off R.J. Sim (RNZAF)	23	Missing	BR 319	Spitfire VI	Shipping strike, flak	5 NE, Sark
29.06.43	Fg Off A. Drew		Safe	BR 314	Spitfire VI	Escort. Bale out	
16.08.43	Fg Off M.H.F. Cooper		Evaded	BR 987	Spitfire VI	Ramrod. Bale out	30 SE, Le Havre

Date	Name	Age	Status	Aircraft	Serial	Cause	Location
22.08.43	F.Sgt R.T. Wright (RAAF)		Safe	Spitfire VI	BS 115	Ditched	4 S, Christchurch
31.08.43	F.Sgt R. McKillop	23	Missing	Spitfire VI	BS 117	Combat. Shot down	Ile de Batz
31.08.43	Sgt P.W. Shale	20	Missing	Spitfire VI	BR 329	Combat. Shot down	Ile de Batz
21.10.43	Plt Off A.F. Smith (RAAF)	20	Killed	Tiger Moth	DE 481	Low flying	Ringwood
05.11.43	Sgt W. Gordon	21	Missing	Spitfire VII	MB 929	Patrol. Ditched	10 SW, Portland
03.12.43	F.Sgt F.W. Rutherford	22	Died of Inj	Spitfire VII	MB 930	Crash landing	Exeter A/F
1944							
21.01.44	Fg Off A.K. Doulton		POW	Spitfire VII	MB 913	FTR	Cambrai
01.04.44	F.Sgt D.E. Johnston (RAAF)	21	Killed	Spitfire VII	MD 116	Scramble. Crashed	Nr Tangmere
22.04.44	WO D.P. Kelly (RAAF)	20	Wounded	Spitfire VII	MB 767	Flak	Nr Cherbourg
22.05.44	Plt Off G.E. Prouting	22	KIA	Spitfire VII		Rhubarb. Flak	Folligny Marsh Yards
07.06.44	Fg Off G.N. Hobson		Safe	Spitfire		Rodeo. Flak	Guingamp
10.06.44	Flt Lt M.A. Graves DFC		Injured	Spitfire VII	MD 104	Rhubarb. Ditched	40 S, Start Point
12.06.44	Flt Lt G.A. Harrison	24	KIA	Spitfire VII	MD 121	Rodeo.Me 109	SE Fougeres
12.06.44	Flt Lt J. McG Cleland (RNZAF)		Safe	Spitfire VII	MB 768	Rodeo. Flak Bale out	12 miles off coast
19.06.44	W.O.R.A. Hart (RAAF)	21	KIA	Spitfire VII	MD 133	Ship recce. Crash	30 SE Start Point
29.06.44	Sgt V.J.T. Allen	20	Killed	Spitfire VII		Low flying	Over home Herefordshire
11.07.44	Fg Off M.H.F. Cooper		Wounded	Spitfire VII	MD 178	Rhubarb. Flak	Angers
15.08.44	W.O. D.A. Gregg	21	Killed	Meteor I	EE 226	Patrol. Crashed	Little Chart A/F
29.08.44	Wg Cdr A. McDowall DFM*		Safe	Meteor I	EE 222	Patrol. Crash land	3 S, Manston
1945							
29.04.45	Sqn Ldr L.W. Watts DFC	28	Killed	Meteor III	EE 273	Patrol. Mid-air	Nr Luneberg
29.04.45	WO B. Cartmel	24	Killed	Meteor III	EE 252	Patrol. Mid-air	Nr Luneberg
Post War							
13.06.48	Fg Off J. McCairns/AC2 Shaw		Killed	Mosquito XXX	NT 423	Crashed on approach	Finningley
11.12.52	Flt Lt B. Kneath DFC		Killed	Meteor F 8	WH 455	Mid Air	North Sea
11.12.52	Flt Lt J.W. Harland		Killed	Meteor F 8	WH 473	Mid Air	North Sea
03.07.53	Sgt A.A. Smith		Killed	Meteor F 8	WF 862	Dived into sea	Valetta, Malta
27.09.53	Plt Off G. Furness		Killed	Meteor F 8	WE 912	Ejected too low	Spalding
22.05.54	Flt Lt H. Blow DFC		Killed	Meteor F 8	WH 278	Lost in cloud	near Sandtoft

BIBLIOGRAPHY

Published Sources

Brickhill, Paul, *Reach for the Sky*, Collins, 1954
Burns, Michael G., *Bader, The Man and his Men*, Arms and Armour, 1990
Crawley, Aidan, *Escape from Germany*, HMSO, 1985
Dundas, Hugh, *Flying Start*, Stanley Paul, 1988
Foreman, John, *Fighter Command War Diaries*, Air Research Publications, 2001
Franks, Norman, *RAF Fighter Command*, Patrick Stephens Ltd, 1992
Franks, Norman, *Air Battle Dunkirk*, Grub Street, 2000
Gray, Colin, *Spitfire Patrol*, Hutchinson, 1990
Hunt, Leslie, *Twenty-One Squadrons*, Garnstone Press, 1972
James, T.C.G., *The Battle of Britain*, Frank Cass, 2000
Johnson, Johnnie, *Wing Leader*, Chatto & Windus, 1956
Mason, Francis K., *Battle Over Britain*, Aston Publication, 1990
Pitchfork, Graham, *Shot Down and on the Run*, National Archives, 2003
Sarkar, Dilip. *Bader's Tangmere Spitfires*, Patrick Stephens Ltd, 1996
Shacklady, Edward, *The Gloster Meteor*, Macdonald & Co., 1962

Official Records

AIR 27/2126 & 2127
AIR 50/176, 402
AIR 208/3341, 3344, 3345, 3347
London Gazette

INDEX

Personnel Index